FROM REVILED TO RESPECTED
A SUPPORTER'S JOURNEY
LEEDS UNITED, 1986-1987

FROM REVILED TO RESPECTED

A SUPPORTER'S JOURNEY

LEEDS UNITED, 1986-1987

NEVILLE COPLEY

Copyright © 2022 Neville Copley

The moral right of the author has been asserted.

Apart from any fair dealing for the purposes of research or private study, or criticism or review, as permitted under the Copyright, Designs and Patents Act 1988, this publication may only be reproduced, stored or transmitted, in any form or by any means, with the prior permission in writing of the publishers, or in the case of reprographic reproduction in accordance with the terms of licences issued by the Copyright Licensing Agency. Enquiries concerning reproduction outside those terms should be sent to the publishers.

Matador
Unit E2 Airfield Business Park,
Harrison Road, Market Harborough,
Leicestershire LE16 7UL
Tel: 0116 279 2299
Email: books@troubador.co.uk
Web: www.troubador.co.uk/matador
Twitter: @matadorbooks

ISBN 978 180313 292 1

British Library Cataloguing in Publication Data.
A catalogue record for this book is available from the British Library.

Printed and bound in the UK by TJ Books Limited, Padstow, Cornwall
Typeset in 11pt Minion Pro by Troubador Publishing Ltd, Leicester, UK

Matador is an imprint of Troubador Publishing Ltd
Photographs copyright, Andrew Varley photography.

MIX
Paper from responsible sources
FSC® C013056

ANY RANDOM WEEKDAY BETWEEN 1984 AND 1987

The job interview wasn't going particularly well. They rarely did in the north of England under Margaret Thatcher's government. I was underqualified for and unsuited to the post of optical technician, but I applied for virtually anything to fake my interest and remain able to claim the benefits that in the mid 1980s had become a necessity for a listless teenager with few prospects.

To be fair to the interviewer, a pleasant man of early middle age, he was paying me more courtesy than I deserved. Patiently, he went through the process of telling me about a position he had no intention of offering me and I had no intention of accepting in the unlikely event that he did want a sullen teenager with no design qualifications to make glass lenses for him. I sat adjacent to him in a chair clearly designed for eye testing and batted away his questions with as much civility as I could muster whilst trying to hide my complete lack of interest. We both had better things to do – well, he probably had, anyway – and I had no wish to take up any more of his time than I had to.

It was time to cut the meeting short in the tried-and-trusted fashion. "OK, that's as much as I have to tell you about the job – do you have any questions?"

"Just one: would I be required to work Saturdays?" I asked.

"Yes, up to 1pm. Is that a problem?"

"Oh, no problem; I just like to go watch Leeds United on Saturday afternoons."

His countenance changed from weary indifference to open contempt. "Oh, you watch that rubbish, do you?"

"Each to their own. They may be rubbish, but they are my rubbish," I retorted, rolling my eyes at the inane, predictable comment; about the eighth of this nature I'd heard that week.

"I suppose if we give you this position, you'll be late every Monday morning while you wait to be released from the cells?" This guy had obviously missed his vocation. With such searing wit, how was he not doing stand-up?

I bridled. "Some of us do go for the football. I know you think that is unusual, but it does happen."

"Yes, well, I have other candidates to see, so unless you have any more questions, we'll finish here and we'll be in touch."

Yes, of course he would. At least I'd saved him the bother of showing me around.

This isn't a totally verbatim conversation – it is cobbled together from the numerous interviews I attended around that time – but the context is ultimately the same. Following Leeds United in the 1980s was a thankless task. The team had excelled in mediocrity for over a decade and had a following whose reputation was renowned throughout the country for violence. Although among a significant minority – if you can forgive the oxymoron – the reputation was largely deserved, we were all labelled with it however little we contributed to the trouble. Being unemployed, a teenager, and a supporter of a football club famous for hooliganism, falling into the role of social pariah was, for me, easy. I was apathetic yet deemed violent, personally oversensitive yet with little empathy for others, lacking in drive in one area yet excessively passionate in another. It was a pigeonhole but, paradoxically, a wide and varied one. A lot of it was fair: I *was* lazy and uninterested in just about anything that didn't involve football or chasing girls.

My only experience of regular paid work had left me unimpressed. A few months after leaving school, I'd winged my way into computer programming via a Youth Training Scheme. For those unfamiliar with this '80s innovation, the Tory government decided to get school leavers out of the unemployment figures by offering all sixteen- and seventeen-year-olds a position on a year-long training scheme which paid the princely sum of twenty-five quid a week (approximately sixty pence an hour). In those days the concept of a minimum wage would have been regarded as outrageous blue-sky thinking. The scheme had the added bonus of providing cheap labour for local companies with no promise of a permanent job after the training period finished.

After my initial astonishment at acquiring the position, I stuck it out for eight months but proved to be as competent in the job as many Leeds United signings of the time were in theirs. I was hopelessly out of my depth and lacked interest. Therefore, my experience ended badly with my rightful dismissal. This was partly due to my reluctance to actually turn up, but the fact that I had zero aptitude for technology didn't help either. In my present job, my status as the company Luddite is legendary. Watching me struggle to master even the most basic of tasks, my colleagues are staggered that I started my working life as a computer programmer. I was neither bothered about the loss of that job, nor keen to take another. On unemployment benefit I received only three pounds a week less than I'd been paid at work. Factor in transport costs and working paid less. At eighteen I lacked the foresight to see that sticking it out would lead to a better, well-paid job with a promising future, and decided that a life on unemployment benefit topped up by the occasional side job would be more lucrative. If anyone asked me what I did I used the vague retort of "Freelance worker subsidised by the government."

Many years later it became almost cool to be unemployed, especially around the time of the financial crisis of 2008 and the resulting credit crunch. As businesses folded empathy was in abundance for those out of work, and even the long-term unemployed managed to find sympathy. But that was not how things worked in the '80s, when many people could remember the days of full employment and Harold Macmillan's 1957 "never had it so good" speech. Children were brought up differently – from the late '90s onwards, everyone was Mummy and Daddy's little star and nothing was going to be beyond them, however mediocre their talents. Ability was no substitute for entitlement. The '80s and early '90s perhaps approached this better, with children told that hard work was the way to get along in the world and, if you've got the talent, go for it. I caught the tail end of the 'you are useless and will never amount to nothing, no matter what you do' parenting style. Yes, the double negative is deliberate on my part and was unintentional on theirs, but nevertheless accurate. How heartily my family laughed when for my nineteenth birthday a girlfriend bought me a book titled *101 Uses for the Unemployed*. It contained a series of crude drawings of unemployed people in humiliating positions, helping the community by being used as doormats for entry into public buildings, or crash test dummies.

Political correctness was still a distant concept in 1986 and my extended family were never slow to undermine my already fragile confidence. I was always told I was going to be a degenerate dropout who would amount to nothing, and I saw no reason to disappoint anyone. Those who have seen the old movie *Billy Liar*, based on the book by local boy Keith Waterhouse, or even the relationship between Jim and Antony Royle in the TV sitcom *The Royle Family*, will understand, as will many working-class teenage boys of the time who had more to say than they had to offer. Both dramas featured young men with aspirations who were constantly put down by contemptuous, disparaging fathers. As I said earlier, for me the derision came more from extended family, but both characters really resonate with me – well, their aspirations apart, but I'm sure you get the point. So the stereotype for me was fair but with reasons. In Waterhouse's book and movie, Billy proved his father right and ended up as a lazy, gutless dreamer. When presented with the chance to run off to London with his one true love (played in the movie by Julie Christie), he bottled it and ran home. I did allow myself a wry, knowing smile, though, when in the later episodes of *The Royle Family* Antony became the successful one while the rest remained opinionated losers. It was especially poignant when his father, the main protagonist of the unrelenting vitriol, sidled up to him and sheepishly asked him for fifty quid so he could go to The Feathers that night. I'm not a religious man, but sometimes the meek do inherit the earth. I am still the only graduate in my family and, despite my moderate achievements, our one success story. I'm not sure of whom this is a more telling reflection.

So what drives a teenager, whose peers crave popularity, to deliberately set himself up to be vilified? There are myriad reasons. At school bullying was a distressing daily occurrence for many, not just me, and at home unintentional mental abuse was as regular as bedtime. These were both huge factors in my deliberate self-isolation. Having a mother who suffered from mental illness and told me regularly that I would be stabbed to death by a gang of boys on my way to school did nothing for my own state of mind or self-confidence. The fact that every night I came home in perfect health did nothing to diminish her conviction, and this nightmarish Groundhog Day continued until I left school. Most people have endearing memories of their mother nurturing them lovingly through their youth with unconditional devotion. These are often related with touching sentiment on social media, and it is of course perfectly correct to recall such memories in this fashion. We all need to remember the good times and cherish them. My most prominent memories of my mother are of her being convinced that Interpol were speaking to her through the bedroom wall, and that they'd kidnapped the real me and put a clone in my place. It was totally perplexing for my few friends to witness my mother demanding to know what I'd done with me and where I was holding me. Another memorable occasion occurred when I was about seventeen and entertaining a girlfriend at home. Although she suffered horribly from her mental illness, my mother also had an extremely cruel sense of humour; something I'm proud to have inherited. Just as I was about to get adventurous with the girl, my mother thought it would be a great idea to charge into my bedroom holding a pair of my pyjama bottoms up to the light and declare that she had no idea what I'd been doing but there was no way she was going to be able to get those stains out. Suitably horrified, the girl made her excuses and left. I never saw her again; I really can't understand why. This piece of inventive satire was compounded by the irony that I cannot recall my mother ever washing anything in her life. I have no doubt that she did when my siblings were young, but due to her illness, by the time I came along (I'm the youngest by thirteen years) she was wholly incapable of any kind of housework. Whilst I was furious I was also impressed by her ingenuity, and I'm still waiting for an opportunity to play that trick myself when I'm too old and infirm to be held responsible.

Anyway, with such an unpredictable home life it was natural for me to seek sanctuary elsewhere. The fact that my chosen refuge was (at least for others) perhaps one of the most dangerous places in Yorkshire and the one place where I was likely to get stabbed by a gang of lads was wonderfully contradictory, but Elland Road was the one place I felt at home. Curiously, my mother never showed any undue concern about my mixing with a group of people with such violent tendencies every Saturday afternoon. I guess she thought I wouldn't make it to the weekend anyway.

In a way, I was attracted by the hatred that has always been prevalent around the club. The thing is, Leeds United was really hated at that time. This may come as a shock to younger people who are now witnessing the recent 'Bielsa Ball' revolution and the kudos it carries. For those of us who were around before it this new-found adulation is perplexing and unnerving in equal measure, but also a pleasant change from the former vitriol. At the time, though, the spite was relentless, and as the club had just experienced their dramatic fall from grace, going from European giants to First Division also-rans in a few short years, there was plenty of mickey-taking glee from the general public. Even on mainstream TV shows unconnected to sport you would regularly hear disparaging remarks. Comedians also found us to be decent fodder when they'd run short of mother-in-law jokes. I remember visiting the Butlin's holiday camp in Filey (the Costa del Sol for the lower working class) in 1980 and going to watch a show. Despite Leeds United's demise being old news by then, the resident comedian dedicated a good two minutes of his set to an assassination which generated howls of laughter from the mainly north-eastern audience. Maybe Butlin's could have found a job for the interviewer I encountered at the optician's; he would have fitted right in. Anyone who suggests that the perceived hatred was just paranoia never lived through it.

I'd always taken hatred to be a personal thing. I understood the reasons why I was a subject of contempt. I came from a poor family living in a half-private, half-council estate, but went to school in leafy upper-working-class Calverley, which meant I stood out somewhat. My hand-me-down clothes were an obvious factor, as was the fact that, when we went back to school after the summer and everyone was asked to write about their holiday, it took every strand of my literary imagination for me to come up with something remotely credible. A half-day trip to Pudsey Park didn't really cut it amongst all the foreign jaunts and British seaside frivolity. I was a Billy Casper in a school of William Browns.

Many people have psychological scars from always being the last to be picked for playground football matches. This, for some, goes a long way towards giving them an irrational dislike of sport. Mine goes a little deeper than that. My earliest memory of playing football (I was about nine at the time) is lining up with twenty or so other boys in the school playground at break time and being picked first – not as the best player, but as the only boy who would not be allowed to play. Quite why one nondescript nine-year-old was allowed to make that decision and none of the others questioned it is open to debate. Perhaps the other boys were just relieved that it wasn't them and felt unable to speak up. Then again, who has the courage or is erudite enough at nine years old to see such unfairness and stand by their peer? Nine is way too young to suffer such extreme social exclusion, and I was suitably scarred (as any boy would be) by that experience, to the point where I still find acceptance bewildering and a little hard to deal with. I bear no malice towards my peers, nor even a great deal towards the perpetrator; children can be cruel. I can't help wondering, though, what happened to him – politics seems the ideal pathway for a trainee sociopath, but I never came across him again after primary school.

This exclusion at school meant that I spent a lot of time playing football on my own at home. We had a big garden and the windowless side of the house backed onto a major part of it. There was a hedge just to the right and an open space to the left, and I used the wall to rebound shots to myself and improve my goalkeeping reflexes. This meant hitting everything to my left to avoid bursting the ball and shredding my skin on the thorns of the unforgiving bushes. The outcome was Peter Bonetti-class shot-stopping skills for anything coming towards my left, but I wouldn't have been able to stop a pig in a passage going to my right. I did occasionally get to play with some kids from the estate, but they were much older than me and their powerful shooting left me with fingers that can still bend back at ridiculous angles as I was too stupid to think about getting out of the way. Those opportunities were few, though, and I spent a lot of time on my one-dimensional back-garden training.

The other problem was that my father was a security guard and often walked the streets in his uniform. Most of my peers on the estate thought he was a police officer. Now, although I went to school in a moderately affluent area, I lived in a poorer area halfway between Rodley and Calverley, and for obvious reasons having a perceived copper as a father brought its own problems and exclusion. Although it meant more financial problems and further exacerbated my Billy Casper role, I was relieved when in the mid '70s he retired. Children have cruel minds but short memories. So basically, my father was in his sixties (not thirties or early forties, as many of my peers' fathers were) and believed to be a police officer, my mother was barking mad, and I wore my clothes until they fell off my back. I was not a strong candidate for social inclusion. The Bullingdon Club was probably not my calling. It wouldn't be fair to apportion blame; my parents did their best with what they had, and I'm grateful to my father for his liberal-for-the-time attitude, which I took with me into adulthood.

The problem was that I stood out. In a way it would have been better to come from one of the poorer estates where everyone was the same; at least I wouldn't have stood out so much and I would have been just another '70s child from a poor home. Having lived on those estates in later times, though, I'm glad I didn't. Though there were good people there the sense of defeat was palpable, and I had no wish to feel such despair. My football team provided me with plenty of occasions to taste defeat without taking it home. However, my upbringing did give me a problem I took into adulthood: I don't really feel like I belong anywhere. I suppose it makes for the utopian liberal ideal of being totally classless. This works for me today and I love being the itinerant maverick but it took a long time to get accustomed to. Over the past nine years I've taught English as a second language across four continents, rarely returning home, and at least when I'm living in different cultures I'm not meant to be a part of things. When you don't belong in the place you call home you are in trouble; so Elland Road and all its manifest problems became the closest thing I had to home during my teens. I wasn't hated even though I thought I was, but I wasn't accepted either. Perhaps 'contempt' would be a more suitable term. In school and at home I stood out for all the wrong reasons. I needed somewhere I could disappear. For me it was a positively enriching experience to find that there was a place where twenty thousand or so others were derided just as much as I was, and I could blend in and become anonymous.

My first memory of Leeds United dates from before my first experience of peer exclusion. I was six years old when in 1973 Leeds played Sunderland in the FA Cup final. Leeds were the incumbent cup holders, strong favourites, and expected to win comfortably against a team from the Second Division. I remember being out in the village that morning and witnessing how neighbours were embracing the day – '70s FA Cup finals enveloped people, with lots of white, yellow and blue, and undiluted optimism wherever one went. My overriding memory, though, is watching the game with my father and witnessing his undisguised smirk as Ian Porterfield scored an early and winning goal for Sunderland. My father was a rugby league man and never really took to football, but even he decided to take the side of the underdog rather than that of his local team. At six years old, and this being my first exposure to football, I was unaware of the significance of the game, the club's reputation or my father's smirk.

As I got older and started to get into football and Leeds United, I began to see the negativity. By 1975 I was a huge fan, and that year's infamous European Cup final debacle had me in tears at the frustration and injustice of it; a state which was only compounded by my father's complete indifference. It was around this time that I began to suspect that there was a real hostility towards my club. The hatred on TV was expected as it generally came from outsiders, but Leeds United were even hated in their own city to a degree. There are many reasons for this. The hatred between followers of opposing teams is patently obvious to anyone with a reasonable grasp of football. The '60s and '70s Leeds United team encompassed the fatal combination of being brilliant and brutal. These two attributes induced jealousy and disgust in equal measure amongst those who didn't share our values. The '80s teams were simply woeful and the supporters, not wishing to feel left out, took over the team's reputation for brutality and took it onto the terraces, sparking both fear and loathing all over the country. In the '80s, whilst the feelings of disgust remained, the jealousy was replaced with outright derision. Although I strenuously denied it at the time, these negative feelings were not without foundation and not quite as perplexing as I led people to believe. When you've got somewhere you are accepted unconditionally you defend it to the death, no matter how much evidence there is to the contrary. You develop a pack-like siege mentality. It's easy to see how others who have equally acute social problems fall into the clutches of religious cults and fail to see the exploitation involved. Unlike cult members, though, football fans can see how the club mercilessly exploits us, disregards our thoughts and opinions, and appears to show us nothing but contempt. I am struggling to think of any other environment where paying customers are treated thus. We see it as a small price to pay, though, and we occasionally get something back, albeit fleetingly, through the odd freak positive result. The consumption and belonging are what matters, and although the results matter consciously they don't affect the attendance of the manic obsessive I had become.

I remember returning home from a 5-0 home thumping by Arsenal in November 1980 to see my father's now undisguised glee at my team taking another hammering. He sat in his chair opposite the TV, glanced in my direction and asked what I had to say for myself; an early indicator of me having to take responsibility for the club's actions even though I'd had absolutely no impact on the result. I was having none of it, though, and my teenage petulance and stubbornness showed through. I offered no excuses and merely asked if I could have an advance on my pocket money as we had another home game against Middlesbrough the following Wednesday. Too stunned to argue, my father just handed over the money without complaint; no doubt bemused by my insolence but also, I suspect and hope, impressed by my devotion and loyalty to a cause he cared little about, as was the case with many in the city. We won the Middlesbrough game 2-1 with two second-half penalties and the Arsenal embarrassment was quickly forgotten, until the next humiliation anyway.

The feelings of people within the city are, if anything, more sinister. Leeds is essentially a rugby league city. The Leeds Rhinos, as they are now, are the biggest club in rugby league, and the best supported. They would hate me for saying this, but they are the Manchester United of rugby league and are despised by other clubs. Until Don Revie came along and transformed Leeds United from a poor Second Division side into European giants, Leeds RL, as they were called then, had the monopoly on winter sport in the city. So a credible rival coming along to steal the attention provoked feelings of jealousy slightly different from those of rival supporters. This churlish attitude was, and still is, one akin to a sulking former prom queen rather than an envious schoolboy. There is some scope to understand the malcontented attitude of the average rugby supporter. They were often casually grouped by the uninformed neutral with the hooligan following from the football club, and it's easy to see why a group of people who were by and large much better behaved would be frustrated at being branded with this lazy stereotype. However, that didn't keep them from using the stereotype themselves. Many is the occasion when there has been trouble at a rugby league game and it has been immediately passed off as the work of football hooligans. This can be a credible explanation in Leeds and Bradford, both of which have sizeable hooligan followings, but less so in, say, Warrington or Widnes. Nevertheless, to the present day, Leeds Rhinos and other rugby supporters are quick to use the football club as a convenient scapegoat when their own supporters are involved in trouble. As an English teacher I always encourage my students to make contentious points as long as they can back them up, so let me digress.

The brother-in-law who took me to my first football match later started to follow rugby league. On the rare occasions when we meet, he never fails to mention the time Leeds RL visited his beloved Bradford Northern and there was fighting in the crowd. He is quick to point out that those doing the fighting did so under two banners in the standing area: one with 'Peacocks' printed on it; the other 'Paraders' – the respective nicknames of the two football clubs at the time. I wasn't there, so I'm in no place to doubt the validity of the story, but I have seen something like six hundred football matches and witnessed more than my fair share of violence, yet never have I observed the perpetrators doing so under identifying banners. Let's be honest: we are all susceptible to a little distortion of the past to suit the point we are trying to make. There will even be experiences I relay in this book that others will remember differently. Still, I would challenge any football fan to say that they have witnessed behaviour such as that described by my brother-in-law at any game they have attended.

There have been other occasions when United fans have been held responsible by Rhinos fans for trouble involving their own supporters. After a rugby league Challenge Cup final at Wembley, Rhinos supporters were seen to be involved in trouble on the train coming back and there were complaints to the local paper from those who witnessed it. Rhinos fans were quick to counter that Leeds United were also playing in the area at Watford and the transgressors could easily have come from there. This is a possibility, but it shows how quick the egg chasers are to apportion blame elsewhere rather than take responsibility for their own (admittedly lesser) hooligan problems. It would also make it easier to identify the culprits if Rhinos supporters didn't adopt chants that were started across the city at Elland Road. The Rhinos even come onto the pitch to the famous football anthem 'Marching on Together', written for Leeds United as their cup final song in 1972. The Rhinos' store in the Merrion Centre in Leeds has a banner in the entrance proclaiming the same message. Cases of mistaken identity would evaporate if the rugby club who show such contempt for the football club managed to find their own identity and stopped feeding off ours. I suppose I should take it as a backhanded compliment. Their resentment springs from personal jealousy that neither their sport nor their team carries the same kudos. Perhaps I would be as resentful if I ever took sufficient time to think about them. As Leeds United supporters, though, what is happening across the city in a sport we have no interest in just isn't worthy of comment.

There was another problematic group around at this time. Whenever I met new people and mentioned Leeds United, along with being told to get to Headingley and watch a proper team and game, I was often also told that the person I was speaking to had stopped going when Revie left. These are supporters who followed the team through the good times then disappeared when things got tough and yet they are strangely proud of their disloyalty. They still speak with passion about the good old days and would hate a return to the good times for the present team, or indeed any team since 1975. It would take away the shine from their stories if we had equally good stories to tell.

In both brigades the deep, engrained narcissism is obvious. So, as a Leeds United supporter, it wasn't necessary to travel too far to witness hostility; it was on your doorstep. However, it was as amusing as it was frustrating, and being part of a collective rather than the focus of individual vilification was something I had been waiting for all my life. Over the next thirty years, I embraced it willingly.

I've always felt that the city of Leeds and its football club match me perfectly. Leeds is a city of underachievement, particularly considering its size. Depending on how you draw the boundaries, Leeds is the third or fourth biggest city in the UK, and by some distance the largest one-club football city. When you consider the catchment area the problem is magnified further. If you place a compass on a map and draw a circle to define a twenty-mile radius around the city, only three other Football League clubs fall within that area: Bradford City, Huddersfield Town, and the recently promoted Harrogate Town. In the '80s Halifax Town were in the Football League too, but only Huddersfield and Bradford provided any credible competition. Bearing this in mind, Leeds United has underachieved and is not as well supported as its face value would suggest. In an old programme from the '80s I found an article dedicated to Second Division clubs which showed their level of support as a percentage of population. This is of course hard to distinguish with London clubs, but Leeds were fourth bottom according to this ratio despite being second in overall numbers. If we take into account that a quarter of the fan base comes from outside the city then the point is magnified further. As I've said before, though, we do have a rival, well-supported club in the city; they just play by a different code of football.

Despite stories to the contrary, this was also the case during Leeds United's one significant period of sustained success. Most people have a rose-tinted view of their youth and there will always be a tendency towards exaggeration, particularly when it's difficult to prove them wrong as it was when computer research was still a distant dream. Followers of Leeds United's peak period are no exception. They tell you stories of Elland Road being packed out every week and queues around the stadium long before kick-off, but on average only six games a season reached forty thousand in a stadium that held over fifty-five thousand. In the 1968–9 season, when Leeds lost only two games on the way to winning their first League Championship, only a quarter of games in all competitions reached forty thousand attendees. There were no home attendances of fifty thousand or more. The only time Leeds had an average attendance of over thirty-nine thousand was the 2001–2 season. When they were champions in 1974, they had a similar home attendance to Everton, who finished in mid-table and had to contend with the competition of Bill Shankly's Liverpool. The attendance for the 1968 Fairs Cup final first leg at Elland Road was a mere twenty-five thousand. This was for only the second ever major trophy win in the club's history.

For many there is always a tendency to gloss over their youthful experiences and it's understandable that memories are favourable. Those that are kept that way, though, should be viewed with an air of suspicion. Fans who witnessed those great times lament the decline in standards when they observe the apparent laziness and apathy of today's stars. With passion they berate modern players for their lack of effort and professionalism, but chuckle indulgently when they recall Billy Bremner and Jack Charlton smoking at the side of the pitch during training. They fly into a rage when a modern player doesn't appear to be taking a game seriously enough, but shrug their shoulders when it's pointed out that the late, great Norman Hunter is quite clearly yawning in photos of the team going out onto the pitch at Wembley for the 1974 Charity Shield match. Any player who wants to leave to gain first team football or even better himself away from an average club is deemed a traitor not worthy of wearing the famous white shirt that adorned his heroes. It doesn't matter that Bremner was incredibly homesick in his early days and basically had his transfer request on a piece of string, he used it that often. They ignore the fact that Jack Charlton tried to push through a move to Manchester United to join his brother Bobby in 1962, and stated often that he was better than the club. No mention is made of Don Revie agreeing to join Sunderland in 1968 and the Leeds board blocking the move. In the early '70s Paul Reaney asked for a transfer when he initially couldn't displace Paul Madeley after returning following an injury. Then of course there is the modern legend David Batty, who in his autobiography admits to speaking to Liverpool behind Leeds' back at the end of his first full season. According to Gordon Strachan and Gary McAllister, Batty didn't even like football much, never mind Leeds. If he was injured or suspended he rarely went near the club on match days. It would seem that players who won something are beyond reproach. I suppose, though, that we shouldn't distort cherished memories with facts. We hang on to them for a reason, and as we grow older they take on even more significance as we witness a life slipping through our fingers. Is it any wonder, then, that we gloss over these times and view them as halcyon days of a wonderful era? The football club in Leeds has produced very few moments of real success, so it's understandable that many hang on to the few lasting memories of being the best.

I also feel that there are a good many amongst the armchair brigade who do all they can to undermine the club. These are people who attended two games a season at most, yet they are the most vociferous of the negatives. I find them utterly bewildering. They spend the whole week telling anyone who pretends to listen how poor the team is, and then on Monday morning complain that they proved to be exactly that over the weekend. It's best not to go too deep into the psyche of someone who on Friday predicts a hammering and then on Monday gets enraged about a narrow defeat. They are entitled to their opinion, though, and God forbid that anyone dare challenge them, like someone who took the time to attend the game. It happens at every club, but

Leeds United are known for having more than their fair share of naysayers. Yes, you are entitled to have your say, but your opinion is not law and is open to challenge. Challenge my opinion, go for it, I can take it. Can you? Also, what would happen if your view *was* taken as law and the club listened to you and you only? Well, in the modern game, Kalvin Phillips, Stuart Dallas, Patrick Bamford, Liam Cooper and Luke Ayling would all have been gone long before the promotion campaign, because every one of them was told to get out of our club by you supposed experts whose views must be upheld. So spout your vitriol if you must, but if you think it serves any purpose then you're hugely mistaken. I've seen this kind of thing in action before and it's not restricted to those who watch from home: I've seen it at games too. I remember taking a supporters' coach to an away match at Coventry in the late '90s. Leeds had beaten Manchester United at home in the previous league game and the coach driver asked the steward how he felt about it. He had nothing to say about beating the reigning Premier League champions, but everything to say about the midweek League Cup defeat by Bristol City. This was a game in which Leeds had played for over an hour with ten men and progressed on aggregate to the next round regardless, but the guy needed to have his moment of negativity. My favourite such moment, though, occurred following an away game against West Bromwich Albion in the late '80s. When I got into work on the following Monday morning, a nominal Leeds fan was waiting for me, almost seething that Leeds had conceded a goal in injury time. Now this was true: in the last action of the game, former Leeds player Martin Dickinson had indeed scored for West Brom. The fact that Leeds were 4–0 up at this point meant absolutely nothing to this detractor; nor did my astonished protestations that we'd won the game convincingly.

Then again, we are talking about Leeds people here, and there is no one more adept at finding fault. I suppose there are reasons why I don't live there now. This pessimism could also account for our dearth of sporting talent. We produce very few world-class sportsmen and even fewer music stars. Which other major city, when asked to name their greatest ever music artists, would struggle to get past the likes of the Kaiser Chiefs and the Pigeon Detectives? Even with the famous and incredibly successful Yorkshire Cricket Club's headquarters firmly entrenched in Leeds, Geoffrey Boycott, Michael Vaughan, Darren Gough and Joe Root all hail from South Yorkshire. After Ray Illingworth and Len Hutton, it's a struggle to name any top-class players from the city itself. The notable exception would be Jim Laker, who spent his entire career at Surrey. Considering its size, Leeds has produced very few footballers: an internet search brings up 121 names. Sheffield, a slightly smaller city by population, offers 322. The small town of Ashington in Northumberland has produced over forty, including our own Jack Charlton. Even the great Leeds team had very few players born in the city. The late Paul Madeley was from Beeston, David Harvey a Leeds-born Scot, and Paul Reaney was brought up in Leeds but born in Fulham. The only other recognisable footballer at that time was striker Kevin Hector, who was born in Leeds but spent most of his career with rivals Derby County. Writers and actors like Peter O'Toole, Keith Waterhouse and Alan Bennett add a literary lilt, but we working-class northerners have always distrusted anything as aesthetically pleasing as the written word. For this reason, many local writers decamped to London at the first sniff of success, and who can blame them? I've heard many a Loiner wax lyrical about the brutality of Leeds RL's Kevin Dick or United's Norman Hunter, but not one who could quote a single line from Bennett or Waterhouse. I remember being persecuted in my forties for reading William Blake at work and spending my weekends watching Shakespeare plays at Kirkstall Abbey. The beautiful and historic Brontë village of Haworth is less than ten miles away but everyone who ventures out there goes for the steam trains or the moors. I know no one who has read a single book by any of the sisters. I have to admit that I have only read them recently myself.

So as a reader and a Leeds fan, I never really managed to fit in amongst my peers. Not long after Leeds had their most successful period in their history, there was only one other true fan where I lived and very few at my school. The yellow, blue and white were displayed by locals merely for the day of the 1973 cup final and soon vanished after the embarrassing defeat, never to return. I think for me this was also one of the team's attractions. Perhaps because of my start in life, I've always shunned the popular. Marbles, skateboards and the *Star Wars* crazes passed me by completely and I steadfastly refused to engage with any of them. Smoking was almost essential for social inclusion but I tried it for a month when I was twelve, decided cigarettes tasted like shit, and couldn't afford smoking and Panini football stickers so the former had to go. I've taken this approach into my adult life and have a great mistrust of populism in any form. Part of this, of course, is down to sheer Yorkshire stubbornness, but I often wonder if, had the Leeds United team of the late '70s carried the same kudos as Liverpool, I'd have gone tearing off in the other direction and followed Halifax Town. I've never been a patriot and the England football team leaves me cold. I don't hate it as some do, but my own team drain my emotions enough; I've nothing left to give England. All my passion is focused on the reviled, underachieving non-entity in the north of England that became a sanctuary for this repressed teen. Others craved the populism I shunned. In the '70s there were a lot of Liverpool and Manchester United fans in my class and only one other Leeds fan. He became one of my closest friends before he moved to high school a year before me. He is also the only one of my schoolmates with whom I have any sort of contact now. He still lives in Leeds and is still a regular home-and-away supporter, as is his son. In the early '80s when things were admittedly dismal, only one other boy in my school year went to Elland Road regularly; an average of roughly two per cent. Leeds United and I were derided and misunderstood in equal measure, and we were a perfect marriage.

This story is one of extremes, hence the title. The prologue has given you a rough background for myself and the club, and what follows tells of the unprecedented changes we both faced throughout the 1986–7 season. First, though, we need to go back to where it all began for me.

LEEDS UNITED V LIVERPOOL, SATURDAY 15TH OCTOBER 1977

THE LOVE AFFAIR BEGINS

I first took my children to Elland Road when they were seven and five years old. Adam, the oldest, had some grasp of what was going on, but his younger brother Matthew was way too young and the event bypassed him completely. I think it's a shame that while Adam still remembers the game, Matthew has absolutely no recollection of the day. Whilst neither of them ever showed my unhealthy commitment to the sport, every fan should be able to remember their first game with overindulged sentiment, and I fear that my impatience to bring him along with us deprived him of that.

Being too young to remember had never been an option for me, though; partly due to financial restrictions, but also because of the problems with hooliganism which had reached endemic heights in the mid '70s. I'd been allowed to go to see Bradford City a few times at the previously mentioned friends' birthday parties, but this was a Fourth Division side attracting crowds of two thousand, with little scope for the mindless violence that was going on a dozen miles along the M62. Even though I'd been to Bradford and enjoyed it my heart still belonged to Leeds, and I was itching to see my first game. My sister's husband, an armchair Liverpool fan, took me along for my first visit to Elland Road. I jumped from crowds of two thousand to one of forty-five thousand and was suitably overwhelmed. That is still the biggest attendance I have seen at Elland Road in over five hundred games.

I think what struck me immediately was the level of violence outside the ground. In the '80s and beyond it was much worse, but contained within the hooligan groups, often away from the stadiums, and usually only prominent at the big games. In the '70s, though, fighting at football was as regular as power cuts and three-day weeks, and broke out everywhere within the stadium and outside it. As we strolled down Lowfields Road, every two minutes or so the crowd would part in front of us to reveal a couple of youths rolling around on the floor, arms and legs going like propellers. Later I came to be frightened by these outbursts of violence – I was never much of a fighter – but in my prepubescent years I was wide-eyed with excitement. Few arrests seemed to be made; the police just picked the combatants up and sent them on their way. It was very much like teachers separating kids in the playground. On reflection, my brother-in-law's decision to wear a Liverpool scarf for the game was at best ill judged. Having a small eleven-year-old boy with him probably saved him from attack, but there were a few menacing threats and comments and I'm sure he's made better decisions in his life. I was almost disappointed to get into the stadium as there seemed to be much more action going on outside. We were sat in the South Stand, long before it became the hooligan enclave of the '80s, so we were relatively safe. Nevertheless, I could still see pockets of violence breaking out on the terraces at frequent intervals.

More than anything, I was taken aback by the size of the stadium. Valley Parade, home of Bradford City, was less than a third of Elland Road's size and usually at least half empty, as you would expect of a struggling Fourth Division side. Liverpool, however, were reigning league and European champions and this was the biggest game of the season. It seemed to me that the entire population of Leeds, if not the country, must be in the stadium. The next thing that struck me was the increased hostility of the atmosphere inside the ground. The outright hatred for people you had never met and were never likely to meet simply because of the colour of their scarf was a new experience. I'd experienced it for the cut of my clothes, but never the colour. Taking into account the fact that this was a game against a strong rival but not an outright adversary made it all the more perplexing. The previous home match against fierce rivals Manchester United had been much worse, with many more arrests. From my first Leeds–Manchester United match (maybe my fifth home game) a few years later, I still have the vision of walking into the stadium and seeing a dozen Leeds fans on the shoulders of friends burning Manchester United scarves on the terraces. Even so, there was a real sense of malevolence in the stadium coming from both sets of supporters, which to an eleven-year-old boy is both terrifying and intoxicating at the same time. The final thing that struck me, and something I miss incredibly to this day, was the floodlights. Until the following season there would be only three of them but, being built in the early '70s as the largest floodlights in Europe, the sight of them on the approach to the ground, and indeed many miles from it, became as portentous as seeing the Tower on a trip to Blackpool. I'd been to Bradford for a night game, and whilst their floodlights provided adequate lighting for the match to take place, they didn't engulf the whole arena as Elland Road's huge diamond-shaped lights did. I lived around five miles from the stadium, and on the days when I wasn't allowed to attend night games there, I could still see the glow of the lights on the horizon and it gave me a sense of belonging, however artificial.

I loved the noise and the tension and the way I was able to lose myself in the occasion. When I'm at Elland Road, I'm completely consumed and think of little else. From that first game I knew where I belonged; I had found my place, where nothing mattered except what was happening directly in front of me. It was enriching to be able to clear my mind of outside problems and focus on the moment. It is a shame I could never manage the same trick in the exam hall, but we all have our peculiarities and I was hooked from the start. My absurd memory still retains portions of this game, and I can still play out the edited highlights I've maintained for over forty years.

I remember Leeds' giant Scottish centre half Gordon McQueen heading against the post directly in front of me; me holding my head in my hands in despair, my sister's husband putting a fatherly hand on my shoulder. I remember Leeds goalkeeper David Stewart's almost balletic, full-length diving save to catch the ball in the top corner, reminiscent of the goalkeeper in the popular football game *Super Striker*. I can instantly recall my elation, jumping out of my seat, as striker Gwyn Thomas shot and Liverpool goalkeeper Ray Clemence could only push the shot onto the post and into the back of the net. I was totally unaware of the explosion of noise in the stadium, and that I was in with the Liverpool fans, such was my delight.

Next came the moments that stick with me the most as they are everything that embodies Leeds United. Leeds were in total control against the league and European champions, but it was time to shoot themselves in the foot. David Stewart came to the edge of his box to collect a ball he was never going to get close to. The loose ball fell to Liverpool forward Jimmy Case, who shot into an empty net.

The scores stayed level until half-time but there was an air of inevitability now. Kenny Dalglish missed a good chance for Liverpool but it was no real surprise when Case added another late in the second half to give Liverpool the win. This is the Leeds way: show what they can do and then, just when you think it's all going to be good, they decide to showcase what they can't do. In this case – and uncountable others since – that would be holding on to a lead.

Despite the result and the abject disappointment, I was undeterred and hungry for more. I only got to see two more games in the next two years, before I discovered the boys' pen and the alluring charms of fifty pence per game in 1980, but even before then my obsession was secured, and between August and May only *Charlie's Angels* and the sultry charms of Jaclyn Smith provided viable competition for my attention. By the time I started to attend regularly in 1980, I was completely gripped. Home games were unmissable and I was usually there around an hour and a half before kick-off. I couldn't get in the stadium until about 2.15, but I liked to sit on Fullerton Park's grass banking opposite the West Stand and watch the car park fill and the tension grow. My pocket money stretched to admission, a match programme, my bus fare, and a greasy hot dog in a stale bun from one of the pungent-smelling vans that were prominent outside all football stadiums. How we got through our twenties without clogged arteries will remain a mystery to many of us. For me the hot dog was always post rather than pre match, as when my team were playing I was incapable of eating before the game, such was my fear of losing. This fasting often left me on the point of collapse before night matches, but it mattered little. Likewise the quality of the opposition; I was just as terrified of the likes of Coventry City, Wolverhampton Wanderers, Stoke City and Brighton & Hove Albion as I was of Liverpool, Manchester United and eventual champions Aston Villa. My fear of supposed weaker sides was justified as Leeds managed to lose away to both Coventry and Brighton, and home and away to Wolves and Stoke. Yet they lost only two games against the teams in the top five home or away, and were unbeaten against Liverpool,

Manchester United, Tottenham Hotspur, and runners-up Ipswich Town. They also beat European Champions Nottingham Forest at Elland Road. Good or bad, reputations meant nothing. From this season on my schoolwork declined rapidly. Monday to Wednesday was spent either lamenting defeat or basking in glory depending on how the previous weekend had gone (usually the former). Thursday and Friday were spent writing possible team formations in a schoolbook meant for quadratic equations, and my own personal equations (4–4–2, 4–3–3) failed to impress my sports-ignorant maths teacher. Weekdays were merely empty space to be filled with reflection or contemplation. Only Saturday mattered.

Leeds United decided that the period following the start of my obsession would be a good time to play the worst football in their history. When in September 1980 I started going to all home games they were bottom of Division One. The board had given in to the fans' anger and sacked manager Jimmy Adamson, replacing him with club legend Allan Clarke, who in 1982 did something Adamson had failed to do and got the team relegated. Although this hurt terribly, it was still worthwhile to have somewhere to belong and to have others hurt with me. It was also the perfect platform to feel hurt. I needed somewhere to wallow in self-pity, where my grief was understood, where everyone was hated, not just me. This was a place where we all learned to accept hatred and eventually revel in it. I'm not sure I even wanted a successful football team; abject mediocrity seemed to suit me and I dovetailed perfectly with the club.

Probably the lowest point for supporter and club was a home League Cup game against Chester City in September 1983. I had finished school a few months before and showed no signs of wanting employment, much to the chagrin of my family. Again, Elland Road was the only place for me to wallow in my apathy, and the club had duly indulged me by losing the previous three games;

the last one leading at half-time against the mighty Shrewsbury Town before going on to lose 5–1. Chester were bottom of the Fourth Division and this was at least an opportunity to stem the tide. Again, though, Leeds United proved to be no respecter of reputations, be they positive or negative, and offered the worst footballing performance I have ever seen. Chester took an early lead and Leeds showed that they had no intention of making them surrender it. Leeds' only attempt on the goal came in the final minutes, and such was the quality of the performance that Leeds fans booed the team onto the pitch for the second half and cheered their utterly confused opponents. Interestingly, the players and board were slaughtered but manager Eddie Gray escaped unscathed. Just over eight thousand, the lowest attendance since the early '60s, witnessed the most shockingly abysmal show of footballing skill ever displayed by a Leeds team at Elland Road. Leeds also lost the next game, making it five in a row, and my desolation was complete.

Ridiculously, the next four were all won, including turning around the Chester game in the second leg. Even Peter Barnes, the club's biggest waste of money pre Tomas Brolin, scored a few goals. In the middle of this run I was offered the YTS job as a computer programmer from which I was eventually fired; an offer that stunned my family, but not as much as it stunned me as I was well aware of how little effort I'd actually put into gaining the position. It seemed that things were looking up for both me and my team. We underachieved and occasionally achieved together, and looked as if we would continue to do so as the late '80s appeared over the horizon.

FEAR AND LOATHING IN SOUTH AND WEST LEEDS

I mentioned earlier that Leeds produces very few music stars. Luckily the rest of the nation held their own, as in the '80s music was the only saving grace of a miserable decade. I really have nothing else to champion from those desolate times. The swinging '60s and swaggering '70s were replaced by the ennui of the '80s. High unemployment, ridiculous fashion and haircuts, and a frustrated society with few prospects, especially in the north of England, where in certain sectors manufacturing ground to an almost complete halt. The fashion and the haircuts were at least amusing. For adolescent boys, both are simply mating accessories, designed to attract the equally neurotic and fashion-conscious teenage girl. You wouldn't think the combination of a lemon or pink sweater, Farah pants, a mullet haircut and a porn-star moustache would have the girls beating a path to your door, but it did; I guess it takes all sorts. It wasn't for me, though; now able to buy my own clothes, I went for a clean-shaven look, adorned in denim with collar-length hair highlighted blond. I also had the obligatory earrings: one stud and one sleeper with a gold cross hanging from it. I'm not sure what look my confused teenaged mind was going for. The best explanation I can give is that if George Michael and David Lee Roth had had a love child and dressed him as a fairground worker you'd be on the right lines. I looked no less ridiculous than the culture vultures mentioned above.

The wannabe hooligans, of course, had developed their own style, and took to wearing expensive brand names and frequenting the South Stand. Ellesse, Patrick, Fred Perry, Lacoste – all became essential terrace wear for the ambitious hooligan hoping to climb the ranks in an age of the up-and-coming psychotic. How many times did I hear the declaration "I'll be in the South Stand; you'll be able to see me, I'll be wearing my Patrick cagoule"? Quite a statement when the whole stand looked like a huge Patrick cagoule. I guess even the hooligans needed something to cling on to in a country that had had its identity shredded.

Football in the mid 1980s was in a perilous state. The people's game had fallen on hard times, and this reached a climax in the spring of 1985. That year had seen the atrocious spectacle of Millwall fans rioting at Luton during an FA Cup tie, the tragic Bradford Fire Disaster in which fifty-two people lost their lives, and the disgraceful ending saw another thirty-nine – Juventus fans this time – crushed to death at the European Cup final at Heysel Stadium in Brussels. Liverpool fans were held largely responsible and ultimately all English football teams were banned from European competition.

Inevitably, Leeds United and their supporters played their own part in football's fall from grace. On the last day of the season, with promotion still a remote possibility, five thousand Leeds supporters travelled to watch the team play the already promoted Birmingham City. Following an early Birmingham goal, the Leeds fans, in an act of true sportsmanship, decided to tear up the stadium and invade the pitch, drawing widespread condemnation. After the game, a wall at the back of the stadium collapsed onto a teenage supporter in the car park, killing him instantly. The revulsion was complete and almost impossible to argue with. Birmingham City supporters swore vengeance for the death for years to come. The wall had collapsed after police forced supporters leaving the ground against it and the tragic lad was actually a Leeds fan, but these minor details were ignored and Leeds United were yet again disgraced. Such was the media hatred at that time that a section of the tabloid press printed stories stating that Leeds fans were also to blame for starting the fire at Valley Parade, and this was widely believed until the fire inspector's report came out. The fact that the Bradford game had been played at the same time as the Birmingham game made little impression on anyone with their own Leeds-hating agenda. Whether or not the press were trying to destroy Leeds is a moot point; the hooligans needed no help. They were quite ably destroying the club on their own, and it was clear that something had to be done. In fairness, the club acted swiftly. From the start of the 1985-6 season, only supporters, club members and season ticket holders were able to purchase away tickets, and from the latter part of the following season the club imposed an ID card scheme for this purpose. This had an incredible effect on the behaviour of supporters, with only occasional minor problems and one major one, which will be discussed later.

The 1985-6 season was a dismal one for all concerned. Football was played out to the lowest attendances since the war, in dilapidated stadiums unchanged in decades save for the perimeter and radial fences used to keep fans off the pitch and away from each other in equal measure. The lack of appeal in European football in the following seasons rendered most games meaningless from around December onwards, with only title challengers and relegation candidates having anything to play for. Many thousands stayed away and few missed it. Only the diehard obsessives and the hooligans remained. Some of the older, affluent fans in the more expensive seats still took their places, but the floating supporters did just that. As a result, the hooligans were even more prominent.

One of the reasons clubs have been reluctant to address or take any responsibility for their more disruptive elements is that they are well aware that these people will always make up a sizeable chunk of their income. Any study of hooliganism will show that in the main they come from the clubs with a large following but little success, or fallen giants entering a period of transition. Manchester United, Leeds United and Chelsea had well-deserved reputations for violence when they spent time in the lower divisions. The other well-known hooligan teams – West Ham United, Millwall, Portsmouth, Sheffield United and Cardiff City – are perennial strugglers from decent-sized clubs, with the possible exception of West Ham. Even West Ham, though, despite the odd cup success, have spent many years and suffered a number of relegations disproportionate to their size. Indeed, most of their success has come in the guise of promotion from a previous relegation.

When teams gain a measure of success, the football takes a more pivotal role, attendances increase and the hooligans are less prominent. In the lower divisions they are still there but more significant, and give the floating supporter even more cause to stay away. Interestingly, although violence is the reason supporters often cite for staying away, this claim doesn't really hold water. In 1985–6 Leeds United only had an attendance above sixteen thousand on four occasions. As Leeds is one of the biggest cities in England, has only one club, and at that time had probably the worst reputation in the country, the previous statement seems to carry some weight. However, those games were against Bradford City, Hull City, Sheffield United and Sunderland: the very clubs where violence was more likely to be a problem. Some of this can be accounted for by the increased numbers of away supporters, but not all. Twelve thousand more turned up for the local derby with Bradford City than attended the Shrewsbury Town game where the chance of violence was zero. Also, the game against notorious troublemakers Millwall was the highest home attendance for seven months. So, although hooliganism was obviously a factor in the mindset of the stay-away supporter, it wasn't the primary concern.

As far as the football was concerned, Leeds United lived up to the preseason apathy of the entire country and produced, for the most part, dismal football. Starting as undeserved promotion favourites, relegation was only avoided in the last home game of the season against the already relegated Carlisle United. Popular manager Eddie Gray was sacked after the club's poor start to the season and replaced by another club legend, Billy Bremner, who did nothing to stem the tide initially. The club went through a period of employing Revie-era legends, with Allan Clarke, Eddie Gray and Bremner all taking the job in succession. Whilst the fans were understandably caught up in the romanticism of this, I always felt that the board had ulterior motives. No matter how bad things got, no one was going to shout for the head of an old playing legend.

Clarke's predecessor Jimmy Adamson took Leeds into Europe and had them in mid-table by the following season. He was subjected to constant, vicious abuse from the middle of the season after qualifying for Europe until his sacking in September 1980. Although I've never been one for calling for the manager's head, Adamson was, to say the least, exasperating. He was of course hampered by his talisman Tony Currie wanting to return south to be with his homesick wife. If anyone was a stereotypical '70s footballer it was Currie. Long, flowing blond hair, chiselled looks, and a swagger typical of the stars of the day, who, if we're honest, were all style and maybe not enough substance. Despite this, Currie achieved godlike status amongst the fans; indeed, he was my first Leeds hero. He was the fulcrum of the side, with outrageous skills and a sublime passing ability. As with Gary McAllister many years later, Leeds results were largely dependent on Currie's attendance and form. Family comes first, though, and he had to go, much to the disappointment of everyone at the club. Adamson chose to replace him with Gary Hamson, an unproven midfielder from Second Division Sheffield United. He started to do the same with the rest of the squad, and the inevitable decline soon happened. The other thing with Adamson was his demeanour. I've searched extensively for TV interviews from his time at Leeds and, whilst I'm sure some exist, I can't find any in which he doesn't look like he has just finished a heavy session in The White Hart. He seems to have a permanent grin, and slurs his words constantly. This might explain some of his transfer decisions. As well as losing Currie, he sold Frank Gray to Nottingham Forest, who went on to win a European Cup medal the season after, and dispensed with the services of top scorer John Hawley. Like I say, I'm not one to shout for the head of the manager, but neither did I mourn Adamson's sacking in September 1980, by which time Leeds were at the bottom of the old First Division.

Clarke, who took over from him, guided the club to a mid-table finish in his first season, then got them relegated in the next. I found Clarke's sorties into the transfer market equally bewildering. Leeds quite clearly needed a proven striker; the previous two seasons had featured top scorers with eight and ten goals. The first was Kevin Hird, a midfielder who took penalties, and the second was Welsh winger Carl Harris. There was constant talk of a new striker signing being imminent, and Leeds were linked with every striker in Europe. Clarke even mooted the possibility of coming out of retirement himself, but nothing materialised. Instead he decided to spend close to a million quid on left-winger Peter Barnes from West Bromwich Albion. Barnes was an exciting talent, but Leeds already had a very good left-winger in Scot Arthur Graham, whom Clarke displaced in favour of Barnes and played in the striker role. He brought Frank Gray, now past his best, back from Nottingham Forest, and then to shore up the defence spent close to half a million on Gray's teammate Kenny Burns. The only things worth mentioning about Burns are his habit of spraying defensive free kicks into the West Stand with alarming regularity, and the fact that he was a perfect example of the 'Dirty Leeds' label. Even hardened hooligans brought up on the less-than-savoury antics of Hunter, Bremner and Johnny Giles shook their heads in disgust at Burns' behaviour. His most memorable moment (if you can call it that) in a Leeds shirt came during a home game against Manchester City in the relegation season. After challenging for the ball with a Man City defender, he fell to the ground opposite him and thought it would be a really good move to smash his studs into the defender's face. Yet the resulting red card seemed to surprise him; he trundled off across the pitch and down the tunnel, shaking his head. His attitude was not shared by his team's supporters, who were astonished by his actions. Even this hugely partisan fifteen-year-old who refused to believe that anyone on his team was ever in the wrong just shrugged his shoulders and waited for the inevitable defeat to come (it did). So really Clarke was no better than Adamson: both were better suited to lower-league management. Clarke regularly criticised his players in the press and listed them for transfer in midseason. Incredibly, he also took a holiday whilst the team was in the middle of a relegation scrap. Despite spending two million on players, instilling a playing philosophy that resulted in a reluctance to cross the halfway line (his team averaged less than a goal a game), and taking the club into the Second Division for the first time in eighteen years, I never once heard a single supporter shout for Clarke's head.

Eddie Gray was sacked after a poor start to a season when the club were expected to gain promotion in 1985. Despite this there were huge demonstrations outside the ground at the end of the next game after his dismissal, demanding that he be reinstated. It's hard to imagine a present-day Leeds manager gaining such support after turning promotion favourites into mid-table nobodies. Perversely, in these situations the supporters usually targeted the board and the players themselves. The victimisation of players is not a new, social-media-generated phenomenon.

Bremner replaced Gray in October 1985 and Leeds escaped relegation in their last home game of the season, thanks mainly to striker Andy Ritchie scoring eight goals in as many games just as Leeds looked to be staring into the abyss of Third Division football for the first time ever. Attendances often dropped below ten thousand and the football was poor, but at least the fans were behaving. The fact that the season passed with no major incidents in English football was seen as a small compensation, and England's decent performance at the 1986 World Cup in Mexico gave cause for cautious optimism for the 1986–7 season. If we're being honest, after 1985 the benchmark wasn't exactly high, but there were very few straws for us to clutch at and we grasped this one avidly. For Leeds United it was business as usual: yet again undeserved preseason promotion favourites; in those days the name counted for more than form. Billy Bremner started to show his prowess in the transfer market, and his love of a short-term fix. Eddie Gray had built a young, exciting team that just lacked a bit of steel at the back, but after his dismissal Bremner chose to break up a large part of the squad. At the time this seemed sensible, but hindsight shows it was foolhardy. He chose to dispense with the services of, among others, Andy Linighan, Scott Sellars, Denis Irwin and Terry Phelan. Only Linighan and Sellars commanded nominal fees. Given the sale of popular young players, the dangerous flirting with relegation, and the undercurrent of violence, it isn't surprising that Leeds United claimed the lowest average attendance in their history: under thirteen thousand. Even the later League One years surpassed this pitiful total.

Bremner created other problems for himself at the start. He sacked his old mate Peter Lorimer, who, despite his age, as the season wore on was sadly missed as a guiding influence for a talented but inexperienced midfield. He then thought it would be a good idea to bring in players from the division he was anxious not to drop into. He raided his old club Doncaster Rovers for Brian Caswell and David Harle; a full back and a midfielder, both of whom proved unable to make the step up in class even in Bremner's mediocre squad. He did learn his lesson later in the season and brought in David Rennie and Brendon Ormsby (from Leicester City and Aston Villa respectively) to add some First Division defensive quality. Both were to have pivotal and memorable roles during the next season. Yet again, though, despite almost taking Leeds down, there were never any shouts for the old legend to be sacked. It seemed that old loyalties to club icons stuck hard.

For the 1986–7 season, the talented youngsters who were allowed to leave on the cheap were replaced with ageing journeymen and unproven lower-division players. Jack Ashurst and Peter Haddock came from Carlisle and Newcastle United to shore up the defence. Winger John Buckley became yet another signing from Doncaster, and prolific striker Keith Edwards was signed from Sheffield United. Only Ashurst had immediate success. Buckley's only contribution was a deflected winner against Reading, and he rarely featured after that. Haddock was often a nervy substitute but blossomed into a decent centre back a couple of years later. Edwards came with high hopes and a great scoring pedigree. He had been prolific in the division for both Sheffield United and Hull City, but spent much of the season on the bench despite scoring some important goals later in the season.

Yet I still believed, as did the bookies, that Leeds were nailed on for promotion. This was not through any degree of sporting knowledge; I believed it every year despite all evidence to the contrary. It was simply a concoction of blind faith and youthful stubbornness. I remember early in 1984, after a humiliating cup hammering (ironically at Allan Clarke's Scunthorpe United), petulantly telling anyone at work who cared to listen that Leeds would be European Champions by 1990. I was greeted with snorts of derision, and rightly so, but I was indignant anyway. It's a shame, really; if I'd played it down a little and stated that Leeds would win a European Cup match in the Camp Nou by 1992 I would have been met with the same hoots of laughter. Still, I suppose hindsight is a wonderful thing. So on the day the fixtures came out I bought an ill-fitting away shirt, too small for my expanding, work-shy bulk, and spent an idle summer plotting the destruction of our adversaries and speculating on how many points we would win in this all-conquering season. How many points we would *need* never actually entered my head – why would it?

The first game couldn't come soon enough. Leeds United had been pretty much useless in preseason friendlies; beaten by three goals by both Aston Villa and Bradford City. Nevertheless, I took them as warm-up matches with no real consequences and knew that when the season started, the lads would be up for it and finally ready to end their First Division exile.

LEEDS UNITED V BLACKBURN ROVERS, SATURDAY 23RD AUGUST 1986

ANOTHER FALSE DAWN

This was the first game of the season and my first away game for some time, so I was really up for it. The club ban on floating supporters purchasing tickets for away games had double the impact on those who couldn't afford the outlay of a season ticket and couldn't get near the already full supporters' club. So, at the start of the season, I cashed in an old insurance policy to purchase a standing season ticket and an away ticket for the game at Blackburn. If there is one thing from the '80s I miss it's the prices; it leaves me hugely nostalgic when I remember that I had change from fifty quid.

In preseason, a few of us had decided to purchase season tickets and go to as many away games as possible. My friends being fickle in the extreme, it came as no surprise that I went to Blackburn on my own. From the following season I started to attend many matches alone, with only occasional company breaking the streak. I took a National Express coach from Leeds and set off with fifty or so strangers on the fifty-mile journey into Lancashire. Despite being average at best, Leeds United always took a large away following, and around 3,500 out of a crowd of eight thousand packed into the away end. There were also some five hundred outside without tickets, hoping the Lancashire Constabulary would take pity on them and allow them entry. They were to be disappointed. With Leeds' hooligan element looming large in the minds of all police forces, it was unlikely that any chance would be given to exacerbate matters.

Inside the stadium, Leeds supporters were in fine voice and early season optimism was apparent in everyone present. The first game is essentially the best day of the season for many supporters of underachieving or habitually poor teams. No humiliating defeats, still unbeaten, still in all the cups. Anything is possible at this stage. The official mantra of the average football fan should be 'Pessimists are rarely disappointed', so for most of us this time of the year is the only real time for unbridled optimism; especially for a team who are usually out of contention for everything by the first week of January. Because of this, the partly defiant, partly self-deprecating *"We are the champions, the champions of Europe"* was sung with more than the usual strength of purpose. For those unfamiliar with the background of that chant, it refers mainly to the universally accepted belief that Leeds were robbed in the 1975 European Cup final by a – shall we say? – less-than-fair referee. A dubious disallowed goal and a couple of cast-iron penalties turned down mean that this first (and still only) European Cup final for Leeds has taken on almost mythic status. The chant gives the impression that Leeds are the real champions. I'm sure, though, that there are those, myself amongst them, who feel that its continued use, even in days of abject mediocrity over forty years later, has an air of self-mockery. Whichever position you take, the chant is rarely absent from a Leeds game, especially a season opener when all bets are still on, and this day was no different.

The game passed in the way many Leeds games did. Leeds flew out of the blocks and looked every inch the promotion contenders everyone thought them to be. Ritchie and Edwards both hit the bar and there were many near misses before Ritchie bundled home just before half-time. In the first half Blackburn were outplayed, and half-time was a wild celebration of greater things to come and an obvious portent for a return to the almost forgotten promised land of the First Division. During the second half, however, Leeds reverted to type. Blackburn dispatched an early penalty past goalkeeper Ronnie Sinclair (a surprise inclusion at the expense of crowd favourite Mervyn Day), and proceeded to push Leeds back. Eventually Blackburn captain Simon Barker smashed a ridiculously easy volley past the hapless debutant Leeds keeper, Edwards wasted a decent late chance, and Leeds captain Ian Snodin received a red card for kicking out at an opponent. Surely a sign of things to come, and we all went home feeling the usual abject disappointment. There was absolutely no surprise, though: this was almost an exact copy of my first ever game and many false dawns to follow.

This game's only lasting legacy for me was the penalty. It was nothing special; my memory for pointless detail recalls a scuffed shot going in off the far post. The reason it sticks in my memory is that it was the first penalty I'd seen scored against Leeds live. The previous six had all been missed; probably the strangest statistic of my football-watching career, as everyone expects penalties to be scored. The first occurred in only my third game, and first away game against Manchester United at Old Trafford. I travelled with another brother-in-law and a group of kids from the school he was working at, and we decided for safety reasons to go in the Stretford End. This would normally be a sensible precaution as we would not be singled out amongst the greatly outnumbered Leeds fans, but left enjoyment of the game completely redundant. Leeds took the lead and then Ashley Grimes missed a penalty for the home team, and on both occasions I tried and failed to look mortified. I also failed to feign appropriate glee halfway through the second half when Mickey Thomas equalised for the home team. Anyway, this seventh penalty of my Leeds career was the first to be converted and the only point worth memorising of a dismal second-half showing against an average Blackburn team. We hadn't even made it to Saturday evening without defeat, and another relegation struggle looked to be on the cards.

LEEDS UNITED V STOKE CITY, MONDAY 25TH AUGUST 1986

JOHN SHERIDAN

John Sheridan made his debut as an eighteen-year-old in November 1982; the first season in the old Second Division. He immediately made his name as an accomplished midfielder with an extensive passing range and a fierce long-range shot. This was somewhat rare in a club which had not seen a decent passer of the ball since the lamentable decision by the mercurial Tony Currie in 1979 to follow his wife and head back south. Sheridan debuted against Middlesbrough in a tedious scoreless draw at Elland Road, where two sides relegated from the previous season worked hard to negate each other's already limited talents.

Even so, Sheridan stood out as a raw talent in a sea of mediocrity. He rarely wasted the ball in that first game, the only times being when he went for the ultimate killer pass; one which he grew to find often in subsequent games. As a passing midfielder he became something of a rarity in this era, and thus very popular. Since the departure of Currie, Leeds had become reliant on players who could run and kick (that's other players, not the ball), so having someone with such vision was a rare treat. Despite his youth Sheridan became the go-to man for opening up the opposition. He kept his place for the rest of the season, and although he broke a leg early the following season and missed the remainder of 1983-4, he was back to his best in 1984-5 as Leeds just missed out on promotion.

The following season, however, he was average at best. Overshadowed by new signing Ian Snodin in the centre of midfield, Sheridan looked set to join the long list headed 'Unfulfilled Potential'. The talent was still there but he appeared uninterested at times. He was also petulant and spent a lot of his time bending the ear of the referee rather than trying to unlock the opposition's defence. He wasn't on his own in that team, but more was expected from a player with real talent. We allow the restricted triers much more scope than we do those with sublime skills but less of a work ethic. Sheridan wasn't a trier in the sense of running until his lungs burst; his ethos was to let the ball do the work. An admirable and refreshing attitude, but unlikely to curry favour when it wasn't going his way and his teammates were under siege. This is perhaps a problem within British football: we don't allow these talented players the platform to flourish, and therefore judge them as exotic luxuries. Tony Currie has a mere twelve England caps; Brian Greenhoff and David Batty, players with less aesthetically pleasing talents, have more than three times as many. Even Glenn Hoddle, the one mercurial talent English football had in the mid '80s, only has around fifty. Diego Maradona always said that he would be nothing without the water carriers, and although his comments could be judged as a little disparaging I don't believe he meant them that way and his views have real substance. The problem in the '80s was that English teams only really had water carriers, and so the game lost some of its style and panache. Fitness took over as the all-important attribute and it was sometimes hard to disagree with the evidence that players with real talent and skill were an unviable luxury for all but the very best. George Best and Rodney Marsh had graced Fulham with their delicate, exotic skills for one season in the late '70s. They finished seventeenth in Division Two, avoiding relegation by a single point. These players still existed at the top of the First Division – Jan Mølby at Liverpool, Kevin Sheedy at Everton, Hoddle at Tottenham Hotspur – but they were generally of little use in the kick-and-rush format of the lower divisions. Sheridan had had his time, but really needed to be in a winning team on the front foot. He had little to offer a team fighting relegation. Few expected much from him this season. He was suspended for the first game at Blackburn but returned in place of the suspended Snodin for the first home game of the season. Suspension for suspension – welcome to the world of watching Leeds.

A crowd of just over twelve thousand turned up for the game. This was the first home game of the season on a bank holiday Monday in a city of over half a million people. If there was ever a sign of a struggling team in a city drowning in apathy, this was it. Stoke scored in the first minute, which seemed to justify the general mood, and we all settled in for a long, frustrating afternoon. For once, though, we were pleasantly surprised. Sheridan took over and began pulling the strings in midfield, Stoke never got a look-in after that, and Leeds' captain Snodin, so integral to the previous season, was barely missed. Sheridan equalised with an exquisite curling effort in the first half and then set up Ian Baird for the winner late on. Supporters went home mollified if not totally convinced, but there was much more to come from Sheridan. His long-range effort against Stoke became commonplace as he became an overnight star; so much so that even the mighty AC Milan had him watched. Bremner too could see his influence, and trusted his prodigy so much that he felt able to sell Snodin to Everton just before Christmas and use the proceeds to strengthen the team's weaker areas. Sheridan's role will become clearer throughout this book, but for now it's safe to say that his effort against Stoke proved to be as much of a portent as Edwards' miss at Blackburn.

HUDDERSFIELD TOWN V LEEDS UNITED, SATURDAY 6TH SEPTEMBER 1986

THE HOOLIGAN CURSE

Overall, a 'nothing' game, despite being a local derby played between two mid-table sides. By this time Leeds had won two and lost two of their opening four games. In what was starting to become his customary fashion, Sheridan gave them the lead with a twenty-five-yard free kick on the stroke of half-time. Huddersfield equalised at the start of the second half, and both teams huffed and puffed through that half without even the remotest suggestion of a winner for either side. So why has this tepid, forgettable game been selected for inclusion in an account of a season which provided many more memorable fixtures? I include it because it gives a perfect example of how the seasoned football supporter had come to regard hooliganism with casual indifference.

During the '80s, and especially as a Leeds fan, witnessing violence (or the pretence of violence) had become as engrained in our culture as unemployment, mullets and Esther Rantzen. We attended games – especially away games – expecting to encounter either violence or the threat of it. Against the more notorious well-supported teams it was as likely as rain in October, and it was only absent against the really poorly supported clubs. My abiding memory of the previous season is having real trouble leaving the stadium and accessing Lowfields Road after the Millwall game, unable to move amongst the swell of angry hooligans waiting for the thousand or so Millwall fans to be let out. I don't know what happened as I finally managed to find my way through the seething mass of adolescence and wander off towards Leeds city centre. I suspect the strong police presence had the matter well under control, and that the two sides spent the customary ten minutes issuing absurd threats they were never going to able to carry out before sidling off home to embellish stories of their afternoon in the local pub.

A local derby is always likely to have its share of problems, and this game was no different. For many years Leeds United and Huddersfield Town had inhabited different worlds, often three divisions apart. Leeds' relegation in 1982 was coupled with Huddersfield's promotion to Division Two in 1983, and suddenly, for the first time in over a decade, the teams were on an even keel. Add to this the fact that Leeds had been knocked out of the League Cup at home by Huddersfield in 1983, and that, in subsequent fixtures, they'd gone five games without gaining a victory against them, and the rivalry had intensified. In fact Eddie Gray had been sacked as a result of a 3–1 defeat away at Leeds Road, then the home of Huddersfield Town.

Accompanying me was Darren, a teenager who had moved to the area recently, and with whom I'd made friends. This was his first away match. Although a Leeds lad at heart, he had only recently moved from Australia, where he had lived since his early childhood, and his experience of sport thus far had been confined to cricket (a much gentler and more refined sport) and Aussie rules (far more brutal than football, but at least the violence was contained on the pitch). His only previous experience of football had been the Stoke game, which had been completely trouble free. He spent most of this game watching with amused bafflement as the two sets of supporters baited each other. Towards the end a large contingent of Town supporters left the standing terrace next to us and congregated in the small stand at the other end of the ground directly opposite. I paid this episode little attention as I was engrossed in the game, dismal though it was. Darren, however, naturally lost interest in twenty-two average footballers cancelling out each other's moderate talents and was spending more time watching the increased tension on the terraces. His curiosity got the better of him.

"Why have they all moved from that stand to that stand?" he asked.

I glanced up from the dull stalemate being acted out in front of me. "Oh, them? Yeah, they're getting numbers together to come round this end after the game," I answered distractedly.

"Err, why? Why don't they just go home?" he wondered out loud.

"They're not coming around here for tea and biscuits, fella."

"Oh shit, really? What are we going to do?" His bafflement turned to alarm as realisation set in.

"Well, not just you and I, but the guys in here will attempt to run them."

"And if they don't run? What the hell happens then?"

"It will be an eventful journey back to the train station."

"Oh Jesus, does this happen every week?"

"Bigger away games? Yeah, usually."

That was pretty much the end of the conversation. I got on with watching the game peter out while Darren prepared himself for the worst. As it happens, the running did occur and a few punches were thrown at the front of the crowd, but we were well away from that. We faced a bit of a savaging by police dogs at the train station but, that apart, the day was largely uneventful. To Darren, though, it was carnage of the highest order, and it was hard to tell what mystified him the most: the fact that grown men liked to spend their Saturday afternoons beating the shit out of people they had never met and being savaged by rabid police dogs, or my total indifference to it all. He was right, of course: there *is* a huge problem – in our society, not just in football – when mindless violence becomes as customary as bringing in the milk. We talked about it on the way home and, being the elder statesman and seasoned pro, I patronisingly told him that this had been a minor skirmish and football violence could get much worse. I must have come across as an insufferable know-it-all bore, but we were both soon to find out how right I was.

BRADFORD CITY V LEEDS UNITED, SATURDAY 20TH SEPTEMBER 1986

VILE ANIMALS AND JOKE POLICING

After the fire disaster, Bradford City played their home games at Odsal Stadium, home of Bradford Northern rugby league club. The previous season's fixture at Odsal had been largely uneventful. Full back Neil Aspin scored an early winner to help ease Leeds' relegation fears, and 2,500 supporters shuffled off home happy on a largely trouble-free March evening.

This fixture was to be different, though. Leeds had found a bit of form and had picked up seven points from nine, culminating in a 3–2 home win against Reading after being 2–0 down at half-time. This was the first season of the new play-off system. In the first two seasons the Football League wanted to reduce the number of First Division clubs from twenty-two to twenty. They did this by having the first two clubs in Division Two promoted automatically and the bottom three relegated. The final place was played out similarly to today's play-offs, but with the team finishing nineteenth in Division One playing the third, fourth and fifth in Division Two, so essentially it would be either two up and three down, or three up and four down. This meant that lower-placed clubs had an interest in the league and promotion much later in the season.

The recent good run meant that Leeds went into the game in fifth place against local rivals. Fatally, Bradford Police decided to go against the wishes of the club and allow the lifting of its ban as, in their words, they could "handle any eventuality". As I recall, it wasn't even an all-ticket match; something that was totally unheard of for Leeds' away fixtures. This crass arrogance and ignorance turned out to be wildly ill judged. The Leeds hooligan element sniffed an opportunity, and against local rivals too. They and others turned out in force: seven thousand Leeds fans descended on Odsal and the Bradford Police, and the latter, used to coping with a couple of hundred away fans in the lower divisions, were overwhelmed. Although Bradford fans were no angels that day and were responsible for a couple of incidents that were pinned on Leeds fans, it has to be said that the Leeds fans' behaviour was disgraceful. Quite simply, a good number behaved like wild animals.

I attended the game with Darren and my fourteen-year-old nephew Michael. It was Michael's first away game; it wasn't just the hooligans who took advantage of the ban being lifted. Others decided that this was as good a place as any for a first away experience, not expecting the baptism of fire that made national news for days. I wonder how many never went to an away game again after what they witnessed. This was certainly the case for my nephew; partly due to his shock at the events, but also to a ban by his panic-stricken parents. They had left their eldest son in my care and gone off to Blackpool for the weekend, and only caught word of the violence on the late evening news. It took all my powers of persuasion to stop them getting the next train back, as we were back home by then and perfectly safe.

There was major trouble in Bradford city centre and outbreaks of violence on the way to the stadium. A few service buses had been trashed by Leeds hooligans, although thankfully not ours. We had travelled from my nephew's home in Wetherby to Leeds, then got the 508 Halifax bus which stopped right outside Odsal. It was, naturally, packed with Leeds fans, but there was no trouble. At the stadium everything was fine at first; the only real problem came when a couple of hundred Leeds fans were moved out of the Bradford end and into the Leeds end. This was a regular occurrence; I'd done it myself for the same fixture the previous season when I'd been unable to purchase tickets. However, that day the two hundred were clearly the Service Crew, the infamous Leeds mob known for causing trouble around the country. Their presence was felt in the Leeds end and they were in a particularly ugly mood.

The game was finely balanced. Bradford led 1–0 halfway through the second half, but Leeds pressed for an equaliser. The game turned in a moment, as did the mood. Peter Swan, Leeds' big, ungainly forward, hit the post; the ball was cleared upfield and Don Goodman, a Leeds-born lad but often the scourge of Leeds United over the years, scored for Bradford to put the game beyond Leeds. The last fifteen minutes played out amid a darkening atmosphere on the terraces, and it was clear there was trouble at the top of the terrace behind us. In our pen there was a great roar, and I looked back to see that a mobile catering van had been set on fire. So-called Leeds fans were keeping the emergency services from getting to the blaze by pelting them with bricks, and it looked as if the burning van would roll down the terracing. Fearful, the Leeds fans at the front escaped onto the pitch and the game was stopped for twenty minutes. A group of them then decided to run towards the Bradford fans in the stand opposite and try to scale the fences and attack them. The fences stopped them, but everything about the day was sickening. My nephew, rightly appalled, never attended an away game again. The press were full of self-righteous indignation and for once it was hard to argue with them. Nigel Clarke of the *Daily Mirror* demanded that the club be thrown out of the league, but he did that about three times a season. Leeds United immediately reimposed their restrictions on away tickets, and these remained in place for many years.

The behaviour of the Leeds fans was inexcusable, but what made it much worse was the fact that Bradford were playing at Odsal just fifteen months after their main stand at Valley Parade had burned down, killing fifty-two of their fans. Many of their supporters, although well away from the burning van, were visibly and understandably shaken. Leeds supporters who had gone onto the pitch to escape it were seen apologising to Bradford's manager, former Leeds legend Trevor Cherry. This was a new low even for Leeds fans, and our shame was complete.

Although I played little part in the violence there was an incident which, whilst not part of the riot, betrays my indifference, and also a weakness I have which borders on a disease. On the pitch I noticed a pretty young brunette girl standing with her friend. Although neither of them was in need of my assistance, I took it upon myself to be their guide amidst the trouble. First, though, I had a moment of complete madness. I mentioned the run on the Bradford fans earlier as if I was just an innocent, casual observer. This is being just a little economical with the truth.

We were stood near the halfway line with a group of other Leeds fans when the Bradford fans in the stand opposite started taunting the Leeds supporters on the pitch in the usual palms-out 'come and take us' fashion. This has always looked incredibly ridiculous to me but, suitably enraged, twenty or so Leeds fans made a dash towards the stand and I thought it would be a great idea to go along for the ride, so I ran for the fence at the back of the small, jeering mob. Now, as I've said, I'm not much of a fighter, so what exactly I had in mind had I managed to climb the fence into the stand is a complete mystery to me. Maybe I'd have bought them a Bovril, as they'd not actually set their own tea stand alight. My actions were clearly ludicrous and I realised this as I was running, and deliberately began to slow down. I went from impersonating Linford Christie to looking like I was running through a swamp. The frontrunners got to the fence and, noticing that they were hugely outnumbered by the fans in the stand, decided that the fence was insurmountable and instead stood next to it, baiting their antagonists before skulking off as the police arrived. A few climbed onto the fence but were pushed back by a hail of stones from the home end. I drifted away with them, failing to notice the two hundred or so Leeds fans who had followed us and unaware that I'd been a prime mover in a charge that became national news. My nephew, Darren and the girls were stood in the centre circle, looking totally perplexed by my actions. I found out later that Michael had seen me run off, had no idea where I was going, and set off to follow me, thinking that I was heading for the exit, and only a quick rugby tackle from Darren had kept him from joining me on the front line. Darren's Aussie rules experience had come in handy on this occasion.

Anyway, I decided to be a gentleman and escort the girls out of the stadium and make sure they got home safely. We walked the mile or so to the bus station. They were Leeds fans but Bradford girls, so in fact I was more in their debt as I had no idea where I was going. However, I was puppy-dog keen to make a good impression, leaving the care of my frightened nephew to Darren. I'm all for family loyalty, but you can only take it so far. The brunette actually seemed interested in me too, and we agreed to meet up at the next home game. I'm not sure what she saw in a twenty-year-old layabout willing to desert not just her but his own friend and young relative to help incite a riot he had no intention of taking part in, but each to their own. The point is, even during a sickening and frightening football riot when I should have been totally appalled by and ashamed of my peers and my own behaviour, I could still find the time to try and pick up a girl and then run off and have the pretence of a punch-up.

I guess that's as close as I'll ever get to multitasking. No matter where I am, I'll always be a sucker for a pretty face. Although during my time as a supporter I was never really involved in the constant trouble, I guess I still deserve the derision and contempt I received on the back of it.

LEEDS UNITED V HULL CITY, SATURDAY 27TH SEPTEMBER 1986

THE RETURN OF MERV AND THE END FOR RONNIE
When Mervyn Day first burst onto the goalkeeping scene in the mid '70s he was venerated as the new messiah; a viable pretender to break Peter Shilton and Ray Clemence's stranglehold on the England goalkeeping position. A winner's medal for West Ham United in the 1975 FA Cup, coupled with the PFA Young Player of the Year award as a nineteen-year-old, only served to strengthen the belief that here was a future England number one for years to come. Yet by 1979 Day was plying his trade in the lower reaches of the old Second Division at Leyton Orient and never played a single game for England at any level. He did get back to the top flight with a transfer to Aston Villa in 1983, but never came close to emulating his earlier success. Nevertheless, when he again dropped a division to join Leeds in February 1985 he was seen as a big name and a bit of a marquee signing. He soon became a fan favourite and was a consistent performer. Although the team who, the following season, almost got themselves relegated took their fair share of derision from the frustrated terraces, Day remained largely unscathed. So, it was with a real sense of incredulity that fans took on board the information that he would not be starting

the season and his place would instead be taken by Ronnie Sinclair, a young Scottish goalkeeper signed from Nottingham Forest.

Now, Scottish goalkeepers have long been the subject of terrace and media ridicule (whether this is deserved is open to conjecture), but Leeds had a great pedigree for the best of them. David Harvey became the long-standing replacement for Gary Sprake and was voted Goalkeeper of the Tournament at the 1974 World Cup. David Stewart was his able deputy and famously delivered a match-winning performance in the 1975 European Cup semi-final in Barcelona, keeping out Johan Cruyff and Johan Neeskens. Before them, Tommy Younger was a fan favourite. All three were Scottish internationals, although Stewart gained only a single cap against East Germany in 1977.

This new young Scot, however, didn't impress the Leeds faithful, who, as archetypal Yorkshiremen, were reluctant to embrace change for change's sake. When a fan favourite is replaced seemingly without good reason, their replacement, however innocent, is on a hiding to nothing. Scrutiny is close; comparisons are inevitable. As with any surprise absence, there were terrace rumours regarding the reasons for Day's deselection (fear of litigation prevents me from repeating them here, and anyway they would serve no purpose for the point I'm making), but in the main, supporters were perplexed as to why a fan favourite had been replaced by an unknown, untried youth.

Ronnie Sinclair played eight games for Leeds and I saw all of them apart from a 1–0 win away at Barnsley; a game which was apparently his best in a Leeds shirt. This means, though, that I saw all the goals he conceded, and I can't for the life of me see what he could have done about any of them. That didn't stop the derision, though. Leeds had made an indifferent start to the season and people were looking for a scapegoat, and a new, unwanted keeper was for them a perfect villain. Right from his first game at Blackburn, fans were turning on Sinclair. The two goals he conceded were a penalty and an unstoppable volley, but he was still vilified for his performance. The next game was his first home game with Leeds and a chance to win over the crowd on home turf. But he had the misfortune to concede in the first minute and the comparisons with his predecessor began in earnest. By his fifth game fans were chanting Mervyn Day's name – always a confidence builder – and Sinclair's future was set in stone.

Day was brought back for the Hull game and, in contrast to Sinclair's early concession during his first home game, managed to produce a flying save in the first five minutes. The prodigal son was home. Leeds went on to win 3–0 in an impressive performance and began a run of four wins in six games, drawing in the other two. They were back in the play-off places and the indifferent start was over, and the reason for the upturn in form was obvious. The young pretender had been replaced by the talisman, the man who should never have been dropped, and Leeds produced their best performance of the season to date. In fairness, Day went on to play a pivotal role in that season, but Ronnie Sinclair never played for Leeds again. He was loaned out to Halifax Town and then transferred to Bristol City, where he gained a promotion before finishing his career in his native Scotland with Ayr United.

Would Day have kept out any of the goals Sinclair conceded? As a goalkeeper myself I have my doubts; to me they all seemed to be beyond the keeper's reach. Would Sinclair have replicated Day's save in the Hull game? Again, it's hard to say, but it's not at all impossible. Mervyn Day came into the Leeds side to replace an unconvincing youngster called Phil Hughes, and helped rejuvenate a failing promotion bid. He had a few good early performances in a side that was playing well and made no huge mistakes. Sinclair was replacing a club icon during an indifferent spell when supporters felt there were others more deserving of the chop.

In later years Day would have his bad days. A comical mix-up between him and Mel Sterland in a 1990 home game against

Barnsley almost cost Leeds their promotion, and in the same season a hapless punch during a home game against Middlesbrough cost Leeds another goal. There were great days too, to be fair: Day's save against former Leeds captain Mark Aizlewood, by then playing for Bradford City, at Valley Parade was truly amazing; a save I have never seen bettered. Day seemed to be able to seamlessly combine breathtaking athleticism and reflexes with occasional blind panic, but he was given the opportunity to make those saves and, as a result, was forgiven for his mistakes.

Sinclair, for me, did very little wrong in a Leeds shirt; he was just really in the right place at the wrong time. He may never have gone on to emulate Mervyn Day at Elland Road and his later career would seem to bear that out, but he was never really allowed a proper start either. Talent obviously comes into it, but so does a stroke of fortune, and both played a part in Mervyn Day becoming a Leeds legend and Ronnie Sinclair becoming one of those players you either cannot recollect at all, or who is first on your team sheet when you are putting together your worst ever Leeds eleven.

As a goalkeeper, I'm strongly defensive of even the bad ones. In many a game I've played out of my skin but appeared to have had a bad game because my defenders decided to have the day off, sit back and watch the cabaret as the opposing forwards turned the game into a human turkey shoot. Yet there have also been games when I've been given the Man of the Match award for doing virtually nothing. This is by the by, though – I'm defensive of keepers because they are the ones who cannot afford to make a mistake. Former Leeds keeper Rob Green is a perfect example here. In his one season with Leeds he played very well and he had a great club career. You don't get anywhere near the England team without one. Yet if you ask anyone outside of the clubs he played for, their main recollection will be the error he made at the 2010 World Cup when he allowed a weak Clint Dempsey shot to squeeze past him and give the USA a valuable equaliser. No matter that he later made a brilliant save from Dempsey to keep England in the game, or that Emile Heskey and Shaun Wright-Phillips missed easy chances that would have made Green's mistake immaterial – in the eyes of the nation, Green cost England the game. Mention the name of another former Leeds keeper, Paul Robinson, and everyone will think of the supposed howler against Croatia when a back pass hit a divot as he was about to kick the ball and it sailed over his foot into the unguarded goal. Quite what Robinson was supposed to do about that and which goalkeeper in history would have been able to prevent it is anyone's guess. As a paid-up member of the former goalkeepers' club, when I think of Robinson I forget this forgivable supposed error and prefer to remember him almost single-handedly keeping out a Rivaldo-inspired Barcelona in a 2000 Champions League game at Elland Road.

I've always thought that the role of the goalkeeper is a representation of my personality and how people see me. The goalkeeper is essentially a loner; a true outsider. If his team is playing well he is largely unemployed; he only really comes into his own when his team is under pressure and, even if just for a short spell, playing poorly. The goalkeeper is unnecessary when things are going well, but essential when backs are against the wall. The Sheridan antithesis, if you like. You only have to look at his role when a goal is scored; no matter which team scores it, the outcome is the same. If it's a goal for the keeper's team, his teammates sprint to congratulate each other while the keeper is left isolated to maintain his position. If it's a goal conceded then – after a period of apportioning blame – his teammates trot sheepishly back to the halfway line, leaving the keeper to pick the ball out of the net whether he was responsible or not. If the goal was the result of a goalkeeping mistake then, like all players, he will be keen to atone for his error, but that means another sustained period of attack by the opposition and vulnerability to another concession. Then there is the thinking time – outfield players are more involved in the game and so have little chance to dwell on mistakes, but a goalkeeper can spend long periods with little to do as his teammates seek to redress the balance. Goalkeepers can have long periods of contemplation whilst still needing to maintain their concentration. Some of the world's great thinkers and writers were goalkeepers: Albert Camus and Vladimir Nabokov to name a couple. Maybe it takes a special kind of mindset to be able to cope with knowing that a single mistake will cost your team. This obviously isn't the same kind of pressure as that faced by, say, a surgeon, for whom a single mistake could cost a life. We are lucky in that respect. The pressure is apparent, though, and we are expected to cope with it.

I feel this pressure in my personal life and especially in romantic relationships; a single mistake has often proved fatal. Many will consider this statement to be nonsense, but I stand by it. They were mistakes I shouldn't have made, but especially in later years when I was dating fellow divorcees I found that I was punished for mistakes they would have permitted their ex-husbands to make. Of course, there is an essence here of 'Fool me once, shame on you; fool me twice, shame on me.' But there have been instances when women have admitted that they won't tolerate the same kind of errors from me. I don't wallow in self-pity here; I take it as a compliment: they expect better of me. It does mean, though, that I've been largely single for the past twenty years as I am far from perfect and my mistakes, as they used to be on the football field, are plentiful.

I do feel that I fit the role of keeper perfectly, though. Remote, a little aloof, sullen, thoughtful and – due to a penchant for diving at the feet of six-foot, thirteen-stone strikers running at about twenty miles an hour – slightly mad. I've seen hard men who could put me on my back with one punch visibly scared when attempting to save a goal, shying away from a firmly struck ball, afraid to be hit; whilst I, by no means anyone's idea of a hard man, didn't think twice about trying to get in the way of a ball hit at three times the pace. I remember playing in a five-a-side game a few years ago. One of my workmates got into a skirmish with a huge player on the opposing team and stood his ground as the other player squared up to him. A little later the same player was through on my goal and unleashed a vicious volley, which I got a finger to but didn't prevent the goal. After the game, the guy who had stood up to the hard man came up to me and said, "Why the hell did you try to stop that? Are you out of your fucking mind?" It had never occurred to me to do anything but try to stop the shot, just as it was natural for him to stand up to the hulking fella who'd hit it. Yet he would have shied away from having a ball kicked at him. Maybe it's just a case of giving a hard man a situation where hitting back is not an option and he's lost.

For me the personal insult of conceding a goal is something I find hard to take, and if there is one thing guaranteed to send me into a rage it's someone asking me how many goals I let in during my last game. I didn't 'let in' any; The other team may have scored ten (my five-a-side team were not the best defensively), but anyone who has seen me play will testify that I never let anything past. I know it's simply verb usage but 'let' suggests a more deliberate action. That has never been my way, as a former boss will remember. When he asked me to throw a game in a five-a-side tournament against an important customer because it would help close a deal, I told him he would have to drop me because I don't throw games for anyone under any circumstances. He had to play me, though, as we only had five players. I conceded a late winner but had the game of my life before that and let in nothing, much to the anger but eventual relief of my boss. So, I'll happily dive at the feet of an oncoming forward and get my hands in the way of shots hit at seventy miles an hour, which on one occasion resulted in my snapping every tendon in one of my fingers and being sidelined for six weeks. Yet I won't deliberately allow a soft shot to pass me in order to seal an important business deal that might save my job.

I suppose courage and madness manifest themselves in many different forms and each person has their own peculiarities. But I maintain that there are distinct parallels between the life of a goalkeeper on and off the pitch, and however self-pitying it may sound, people treat us accordingly, albeit maybe subconsciously. This is my theory and I'm sticking to it; I'm sure Ronnie Sinclair would understand.

LEEDS UNITED V CRYSTAL PALACE AND PORTSMOUTH, SATURDAY 11TH AND SATURDAY 18TH OCTOBER 1986

A NEW DAWN; A REAL ONE THIS TIME - WELL, ALMOST

As football violence was a regular, if unwanted, part of British culture at the time, the scenes at Bradford were largely forgotten within a couple of weeks. The police had studied security cameras and made dawn raids on the worst of the hooligans that day and the public disgust seemed moderately assuaged. However bad things get, you move on until the next outrage occurs.

On the field, Leeds were dire in a couple of cup ties and produced their customary early exit in the League Cup. In the league, though, things were picking up. The home victory over Hull and a decent away draw against an unbeaten Plymouth Argyle side left Leeds in fourth place with upcoming home fixtures against the top two: Crystal Palace and Portsmouth. League leaders Palace came first. Although the goals came late – a second-half Sheridan penalty and two in the last three minutes – Leeds were comfortable winners and we started to believe that this was going to be the year. Even Keith Edwards managed a rare goal. Andy Ritchie had missed a first-half penalty after scoring one at home to Hull, but this was

LEEDS UNITED V CRYSTAL PALACE AND PORTSMOUTH, SATURDAY 11TH AND SATURDAY 18TH OCTOBER 1986

quickly forgotten following an excellent performance despite the meagre attendance of fourteen thousand.

Portsmouth were now top and had conceded only two goals all season. As they were probably the best team in the division this was going to be a much sterner test and a better game to gauge Leeds' progress. The team once again stepped up to the mark, with Sheridan in magnificent form. It took another penalty to get them going but they ran out as comfortable 3-1 winners, with Ian Baird and Andy Ritchie adding second-half goals. A crowd of over twenty-one thousand – the largest in almost three years – was suitably impressed and as loud as they'd been at any time since the First Division days. Leeds rose to second and the automatic promotion places for only the second time in five years. The football had been high-octane, passionate and at times breathtaking. Sheridan played like a man possessed and Elland Road became a fortress again. Supporters went home euphoric and dreams of promotion seemed genuinely possible. Then seven points in the next seven games threw Leeds back into mid-table; still in touch with the play-offs, but losing ground on the leaders. Football teams have a habit of doing that: allowing you to dream, then ripping it away with a spell of unexplained mediocrity; beating the league leaders with consummate ease, then the following week looking like a Sunday pub team losing to the bottom club.

I myself mirrored the team's fortunes. I started to get interviews for jobs and the aforementioned girl was prominent in my life. But I never saw her again after the Portsmouth game, and over the next few weeks the rejection letters piled up with the same regularity as Leeds' loss of form. Just like the club, I was approaching my regular Christmas slump, and I dropped back to being my usual uninterested self, much to the disgust of my family and friends. I had the ability to be charming and effervescent and this did happen on rare occasions, but, like my club, for the most part I was unpredictable and argumentative with a penchant for wallowing in self-pity, and as Christmas 1986 approached, neither club nor supporter showed any real sign of pulling out of their slump.

LEEDS UNITED V DERBY COUNTY, SATURDAY 29TH NOVEMBER 1986

RENEWED BUT SHORT-LIVED OPTIMISM, AND POOR ROLE MODELS

To start with, November 1986 was a terrible month for Leeds. Initially it was all hype and subterfuge. Leeds had an early kick-off against Millwall and, if successful, would have topped the league for a few hours. But Leeds' record at Millwall has always been terrible, and a penalty from a young emerging forward named Teddy Sheringham put that dream to bed. A defeat in the next home game against promotion-chasing Oldham Athletic (the third defeat against them in six weeks) compounded the misery and by the middle of November promotion was starting to slip away. A defeat at Birmingham City after leading with ten minutes to go, and it was obvious where the season was heading. Early optimism, a false dawn and yet more mid-table anonymity beckoned. I was heading pretty much the same way. The girl I'd met at the riot had disappeared and I had no one else in sight. My job prospects were even more remote, and I basked in sullen apathy. There was little hope for me or my club.

On the final weekend of the month, there were two events which were designed to fully eradicate my confidence. In the morning I was playing the older, experienced head in goal for a team made up of players a little younger than me. We weren't in a league; we used to play occasional friendly matches, which is why I didn't take it that seriously. This match was against a local side from Bradford who, despite being the same age, were much better and had a couple of players on the books of Fourth Division sides. In the afternoon Leeds were at home to league leaders Derby County, who were flying and taking all before them in an ultimately championship-winning season. With this in mind, and little hope for success on either front, I did what every professional should do and got slaughtered on the Friday night; so much so that I went into the local service station on Rodley Roundabout with a pack of beer to talk to a friend who had been working the night shift. We had kind of an impromptu party and I ended up staying there all night. We were due to kick off at about ten in the morning and our team captain got wind of where I was and, having a new player with him, wanted to introduce him to his senior player. Anyone who knows the service station will remember that they also sold food and had chest freezers in the middle of the shop. So, as my captain came in with the new player, they witnessed their senior and most responsible player lying semi-conscious in a freezer, up to his armpits in frozen peas, looking like a hung-over praying mantis. This was roughly one hour before kick-off. A quick revival session including the captain ducking my head under the cold tap in the men's bathroom, and I was good to go.

Obviously, the potent cocktail of ice-cold water and frozen vegetables had a positive effect on me, because I had a blinder. The other team was indeed much better, but I managed to keep them at bay for the most part and we held on for an unlikely 4–4 draw. Our manager, a local police detective, seemed unconcerned that his hero of the hour was a hung-over goalkeeper of barely legal drinking age and, having expected a hammering, was delighted with the result. I used to meet him in the local pub occasionally and he would always talk about how much satisfaction that game gave him. It was nice to see my drunken antics satisfy someone rather than horrify them. OK, it was my Saturday performance between the sticks, which was in spite of rather than because of my drunken escapades, but in the future it gave me the excuse of saying that I always play better when I'm drunk.

This, however, left me with a problem. We usually played on a Sunday, which left me the whole of the day and, if I'm honest, the next week to recover. Playing on a Saturday morning meant that I had to forgo my usual Saturday-lunchtime pub visit. Since the Hull game I'd taken on The George on Great George Street in Leeds city centre as my lucky local but I didn't have time to get there. Clearly I was going to have to do the unthinkable and watch Leeds play the runaway league leaders sober and hung-over. Not a prospect I was looking forward to; I was used to watching them through a dull drunken haze. I was occasionally euphoric but mostly just drunk and, due to the usual abject performances, melancholic.

Leeds seemed to sense my discomfort and played magnificently. Enter yet again John Sheridan. He'd scored another screamer in the previous defeat at Birmingham and was starting to look like the one crock of gold in a lamentably average season. After ten minutes on the edge of the box, Leeds got a free kick. Ian Snodin laid the ball back to Sheridan behind him and moved out of his way. In one movement, Sheridan flicked the ball up and rifled an unstoppable volley into the top corner, similar to the famous Ernie Hunt goal for Coventry City in the 1970s. Elland Road hadn't seen anything like this in a long time, and everyone rightly went crazy. A perfect performance was rounded off three minutes from the end when Sheridan put Edwards through on goal and he finished with ease to put the result beyond doubt.

I floated home and spent the rest of the weekend in a self-satisfied glow. I'd had a great Friday night, and early Saturday morning had played out of my skin whilst hung-over and admittedly still slightly drunk. I'd seen my two teams claim unlikely results. I'd witnessed John Sheridan score the goal of the season, and Keith Edwards finish a one-on-one. All I needed now was for page three model Linda Lusardi to pop around and offer some horizontal gymnastics and my world would have been complete. This was obviously a watershed moment. Life was going to be a bed of roses for me and my football team from now on, and the early November gloom was replaced by a positive pre-Christmas spirit. December was certainly going to be a month to remember for everyone, and the New Year could only start in the same vein. We were definitely on a roll.

WEST BROMWICH ALBION V LEEDS UNITED, SATURDAY 6TH DECEMBER 1986

BACK TO REALITY

A disastrous day for Leeds: a 3–0 thumping, two players sent off, and some more crowd trouble with a hut at the back of the away end being set alight. The timing of this act of arson was particularly unfortunate as the FA Cup third-round draw was made that weekend. Leeds were drawn away to non-league Telford United, who had of late developed a reputation as giant killers. Two years previously they had knocked out future Division Three champions Bradford City, and they'd never lost at home to league opposition. It soon became clear that Telford would be unable to stage a tie of such magnitude given the size and reputation of the away following, and it was suggested that Leeds fans be banned from the tie. This was deemed unworkable and eventually the tie was switched to West Bromwich Albion's Hawthorns ground; the scene of the Leeds fans' most recent indiscretion.

Predictably, the press seized on this as a victory for hooliganism, even though Telford admitted it was the size of the game rather than the threat of hooliganism that had prompted the decision. There were pompous calls for Leeds to be thrown out of the competition; amazingly, backed by their own local paper, the *Yorkshire Evening Post*. Whilst I would never defend the behaviour of certain supporters, these calls were simply gross hypocrisy. Even at their most violent a few years previously, Leeds hooligans had rarely caused trouble at such places, saving their best for teams with equally bellicose support, and since the ban trouble at these fixtures had been almost non-existent. Except, of course, for the most recent ill-judged transgression, and this gave the media a perfect excuse to jump back on the Leeds-hating bandwagon. Former players decided they too were entitled to voice their opinion, and self-confessed Leeds hater and former Liverpool captain Emlyn Hughes led the calls for the club to be banned, claiming that Telford were being denied the chance of glory on their own ground because of the behaviour of away team supporters. On face value this was a good point, and I certainly didn't fancy Leeds' chances of getting a result there. But Telford clearly stated that it was the number, not the behaviour, of Leeds fans that was their primary concern.

Three years later, non-league Woking were drawn at home in the fourth round to play Everton. Woking decided their stadium wasn't equipped to stage such a tie and moved it to Everton's Goodison Park. Rather than get morally indignant, the press thought this was a great idea to generate a huge payday for the club. Funny, that.

STOKE CITY V LEEDS UNITED, SUNDAY 21ST DECEMBER 1986

MISSED OPPORTUNITIES

Leeds were scratching around just outside the play-offs without suggesting that they would get actively involved. Stoke City had been on a midseason resurgence, so I convinced myself that it had the potential to be a good game and treated myself to an early Christmas present of coach and match tickets.

Leeds had been beaten 6–2 at Stoke the previous season and Mervyn Day went to the press to inform Stoke that it wouldn't be as easy this time around and he certainly wouldn't be picking the ball out of the back of the net six times on this occasion. A very perceptive statement from our Merv, because this time Stoke won 7–2 and were 5–0 up at half-time.

I would have liked to ignore this fixture completely but it serves as an example of my obsession. I never actually went to the match. Due to a sequence of events too boring and complicated to list here, I missed the coach by about ten minutes, skulked off home and had to be content with the radio, which only provided updates rather than commentary. As each goal went in my misery was compounded, but the ridiculous thing is that I still wanted to be there. I felt I was missing out somehow. The average supporter would heave a sigh of relief at missing such an embarrassment, but an average supporter is unlikely to make a two-hundred-mile round trip on a Sunday just before Christmas, for a midday kick-off in a relatively meaningless game. Indeed, I think it was here that Leeds supporters first started to show a penchant for self-parody, chanting, "Next goal wins" when the score was 7–1. When you support an unsuccessful club these moments start to take on a symbolic quality; amusing relief in a succession of barren, trophyless seasons. I've always felt that supporters of successful clubs lack this ability to self-parody, and in fortunate times it has also diminished amongst Leeds fans. Perhaps justly, many of my family and friends accused me of taking myself way too seriously, but paradoxically, I felt a deep sense of loss at not being there to see my team get savaged by an average Second Division side and join two thousand others in taking the piss out of myself.

On another note, I actually got an interview. It was only for a part-time office job, but it was an interview all the same; my first since the ill-fated technician's job interview in the summer. This interview was for a job I wanted and felt I could do, and under normal circumstances I would have been delighted. December 1986 was not a month for normal circumstances, though. It was a month of 7–2 defeats, missed coaches and postal strikes. The letter offering me the interview arrived three days after the interview date. It didn't hurt anywhere near as much as the defeat at Stoke but it did compound my pre-Christmas misery.

How could things possibly get any worse? Well, a poor run of results with only a solitary win over Oldham to compensate meant that Leeds were fast dropping away from the play-offs. This added to my apathy, but there was always the New Year and the romance of the FA Cup.

TELFORD UNITED V LEEDS UNITED, FA CUP THIRD ROUND, SUNDAY 11TH JANUARY 1987

A TURNING POINT

Billy Bremner, Leeds United's famous captain from their most successful period, and manager for this season, stated before the 1972 FA Cup final that he would happily sacrifice all his medals and his Scottish caps for just one FA Cup winner's medal. Such was the romance surrounding the FA Cup.

Mainly due to the financial incentive of the European Champions League, the FA Cup has been hugely diminished in stature. The bigger teams play weakened teams in the early rounds but, paradoxically, usually end up winning it anyway. In the past thirty years only Wigan Athletic, Portsmouth and (just recently) Leicester City have broken the mould of big-name winners. It could also be said that TV coverage has affected the competition's popularity amongst fans. Until 1983, except for the European Cup final and European finals involving British clubs, the FA Cup final was the only domestic match shown live on TV. Semi-finals were restricted to highlights programmes, as was the League Cup final, and even title deciders suffered the same fate. When title deciders were played in midweek there weren't even highlights programmes and it was only possible to catch the goals on the late evening news. So in the '70s and '80s the FA Cup had huge countrywide appeal, and the final itself was a national institution. Even if your club was not involved it was a chance to see a full, live domestic game and, even though the occasion was tinged with jealousy, it was still possible to enjoy it. *Grandstand*, always a dominant force on Saturday afternoons from 12.30pm to 5pm, would start their programme at 9.30am on match day and devote the whole day to it. For reasons of age and safety I wasn't allowed to attend a live Leeds game until late 1977 and only started going regularly in 1980, so despite my team never being involved it was the pinnacle of my footballing season and I loved the glamour of the occasion. The FA Cup superseded the Football League Championship by some sixteen years.

At that time, lower-division teams seemed to rise to the occasion; between 1973 and 1984 three Second Division teams won the trophy and another two reached the final. West Ham United and Ipswich Town both won the trophy having finished in the bottom half of the First Division, and in 1981 finalists Tottenham Hotspur and Manchester City had finished tenth and twelfth respectively. In 1983 Brighton reached the final and finished bottom of the First Division. Only eight of the twenty-four finalists in the twelve-year period had finished in the top five of the First Division, and only one in the top two. A couple of Third Division teams had also made the semi-finals. One of them, Crystal Palace, knocked Leeds out in the fourth round in 1976. Leeds were cup favourites going into the game. Never let it be said that we don't play a part in the history of the greatest knockout competition in the world. The other third-tier team to make the semi-final, Plymouth Argyle, suffered a narrow defeat to First Division Watford in 1984. So we had a competition that was no respecter of reputations. Between 1976 and 1985 Liverpool won seven league titles, four European Cups and four League Cups, but only reached the cup final once. It was a competition that allowed smaller clubs' supporters to dream in a way that the league didn't, and we were all caught up in the romance of it. Also, it's the only competition that starts so far down the league pyramid. The English league is unique anyway, having close to one hundred professional teams and many more semi-professional. The FA Cup starts in September at around tier ten level and allows even part-time footballers to dream of success. In 1974 my local part-time team, Farsley Celtic, reached the first round for the first time and were drawn at home to Tranmere Rovers. They were beaten 2–0, with future England international Steve Coppell scoring one of the goals. It is perhaps this depth that gives the tournament its romance.

I played for Farsley for a short while in the early '80s. I only played for the under-sixteen team and was way out of my depth and far too lazy to embrace the step up in training from playground knockabout to the intense physical fitness required at that level. I remember the first training session and doing twelve laps of the pitch just to warm up. We did not see a ball at all during that first session and I was convinced that I'd caught polio when I woke the following morning. I stuck it out for a while but left after a few months and went back to the local park where I could resume my supreme role of flat-track bully. There you have my claim to fame: I once spent four months being hopelessly outplayed in the youngest (and therefore poorest) team of a club that produced Stuart McCall and Paul Madeley and once had a future England international score against them. I bet my grandchildren will be bursting with pride.

I think it's fair to say that, up until the end of the '80s, most supporters would have taken an FA Cup win over the league any day of the week, which entirely echoes Bremner's thoughts. As he was now manager and had finally achieved his dream of raising the cup himself, he would have loved to see his beloved team win the trophy one more time. Unlikely as this was as an average Second Division team, it had been done before, and recently. I knew, however, that it was something I was unlikely to witness that season, even though it was always at the forefront of my footballing dreams.

For their part, Leeds United usually helped to fulfil my dreams of FA Cup glory by refusing to get involved. Their aversion to the competition was almost legendary. I became a supporter just after the golden Revie age. In that ten-year period Leeds played in four cup finals and two semi-finals. Their record immediately afterwards is almost non-existent. Between 1978 and 1994 they managed to get knocked out in the third round nine times, and only reached the fifth round once. Although this was not a golden period for Leeds, in other competitions they won the league and the Second Division title and played three League Cup semi-finals. Still, it was almost as if they always had a prior engagement on the day of the FA Cup fourth round. This didn't go unnoticed by my friends and family, who knew that my whereabouts would be dictated by the fixtures list. But they could happily arrange something for the last Saturday in January, safe in the knowledge that I would have nothing better to do.

For the 1987 FA Cup I expected nothing different. Leeds had gone out in the third round in the three previous seasons, two of those to Scunthorpe United and Peterborough United, and had not gone past the fourth round in the preceding ten years. When the draw was made and Leeds were drawn away at non-league Telford, a club with a tremendous cup history, the game shone like a beacon as the giant killing of the round. The animosity of even local media whipped the country into a frenzy, and a nation caught up in the romanticism of an underdog could smell blood and clamoured for a home victory even more than normal. For my part, although I'd resigned myself to defeat, I decided to attend the game anyway. The result was immaterial and the consumption was everything, and it was a chance to visit another away ground for the first time. Obsessive football fans are notoriously proud of the number of away grounds they have visited and wear it like a badge of honour; anybody visiting fewer than at least half of the main stadiums is deemed to lack the desired level of commitment.

Due to the mania surrounding the fixture, getting a ticket proved to be extremely difficult and worthy of a badge of honour on its own. After the Bradford riot, the all-ticket ban had been rightly reintroduced and tickets were only made available to season ticket holders and supporters' club members. Added to this, the club would only accept applications by post for this game, which the FA scheduled for a Sunday with a twelve o'clock kick-off, which meant a 6am start for anybody coming from Leeds. They were taking no chances. These early Sunday kick-offs were designed to prevent drinking before the game, and were utterly futile. The lads who were up for violence had the connections to secure a before-hours drinking spot if they needed to, and the association between drinking and football violence is tenuous at best. Traditionally one observes attempts at storming an opposition pub and pride in taking over a pub in an opposition city, but these are territorial actions and their links to actual drinking incidental. The serious hooligans who go mainly for the trouble tend to avoid excessive drinking as they wish to have a clear head when encountering opposing fans. There is just as much trouble at early kick-offs as there is for the standard 3pm kick-off; the timing is immaterial, as is the supposed limited access to drink. The identity of the opposition is important, as demonstrated by the list of places Leeds fans had been in trouble in the preceding two years. Bradford, Huddersfield, Birmingham, Millwall, Sheffield United – three local rivals and two others with a notorious following. Games against Cambridge United and Carlisle United had in recent seasons resulted in Leeds supporters being awarded Best Behaved Away Supporters titles, but these were smaller clubs with a small hooligan element, so it's difficult to see what the perceived threat was from a non-league team with virtually no hooligan following. After the problems of the mid 1980s the hooligan movement had actually started to die down around this time, and anyone who knows anything about the game knows that from around 1988 onwards the hooligans drifted towards the acid house/rave scene and remained there for several years. The threat of violence, particularly with the ban in place, was basically nil. Admittedly, there was always likely to be the problem of ticketless fans but, as mentioned earlier at the Blackburn game, these were simply refused entrance and mooched around outside until the game was over.

If the FA can be expected to be anything, though, it's smug and self-righteous. Chairman Bert Millichip pontificated on the masses of ticketless hooligans descending on Telford's tiny Bucks Head ground, and even appeared to make himself look magnanimous as he selflessly offered the stadium of his own club, West Bromwich Albion, to stage the tie. He would, of course, have done this without the expectation of a rental fee. The country bought into the moral indignation at this poor little club having to change venue because of the big, bad, menacing pantomime villain from the north, and with a resounding boo demanded our removal from the competition. The game would have had to be moved for any fair-sized opposition, but no matter: the antagonist had to be brought to justice. In an incredible piece of bandwagon-jumping, the *Yorkshire Evening Post* became the ultimate turncoat and ran an editorial stating that they hoped Leeds would be knocked out and Telford win the tie. This took treachery to a new level in the minds of the already trodden-on Leeds faithful, and fostered an even greater siege mentality.

Despite the severe ticket restrictions, some two thousand Leeds fans got up at 6am and set off for The Hawthorns for the noon kick-off. My ticket had duly arrived in the post, the local postal strike having conveniently ended a few days earlier. Would I have swapped it for getting the letter inviting me for the job interview on time? Silly question – I joined the other supporters taking the National Express bus from Leeds.

The game itself was terrible. The pitch was covered in snow and ice and, but for the amount of security planning that had gone into it, the fixture would certainly have been postponed. Leeds didn't let the pitch affect their performance, though; they produced their usual abject display when faced with lower-league opposition. Ian Baird scored a fortunate early goal when the Telford goalkeeper slipped trying to save his downward header. Mervyn Day replicated the mistake early in the second half, gifting Telford an equaliser, then redeemed himself with a terrific late save from a free kick. The rest of the game was a comical mixture of misplaced passes and slipping on the treacherous icy pitch. It was petering out into a tepid draw when Baird found himself played in behind the Telford defence and drilled a low shot past their keeper in front of the Leeds fans. The Leeds end became a throbbing mass of shameless frivolity. Not because there was any great thrill in beating non-league opposition or an expectance of real progress in a competition that had eluded them for so long; it was merely to stick two fingers up at the establishment and the rest of the country. The great thing about following a universally hated team is the extra delight when things go your way and you know your opponents and detractors are absolutely sickened by your success. Leeds were in the fourth round for the first time since 1984 and the worst transgression of their fans was our pitiful attempt to sing along with the tannoy to Jackie Wilson's 'Reet Petite', which was top of the charts at the time. Oh, and the persistent jumping up and down to keep warm, but even the West Midlands Police couldn't deny us that luxury.

Around this time there was moral outrage about the injustice of being a Leeds fan. We accepted that our reputation was largely deserved but felt that others were equally culpable, and for them no punishment was ever forthcoming. Newcastle's St James' Park was a horrible place to travel for an away supporter and I've never met anyone who enjoyed going there. Even clubs with more violent support were fearful of visiting there, yet their reputation is one of salt-of-the-earth exuberant passion. Whenever Newcastle are in trouble the media ignore it and the FA sweep it under the carpet. I've been away to every major hooligan team in England – Millwall, Chelsea, Birmingham, Sheffield United, Huddersfield, West Ham, Manchester United, Manchester City, Middlesbrough and Portsmouth – yet never have I been as scared as I was during my visits to St James' Park.

In the '90s when the hooliganism had largely diminished, it became customary to let away and home supporters leave the stadium at the same time. This was unheard of in the '80s, when forty-five-minute delays after games were commonplace. Throughout the '90s I can remember being kept behind at only two places: Manchester United (for obvious reasons), and Newcastle if we won. A friend witnessed Newcastle fans trying to fight police horses in an attempt to get at Leeds fans after a 3–0 Leeds victory. In 1990, when Leeds were again vilified following the last league game at Bournemouth and admittedly shameful scenes around the ground and in the town centre, they were threatened with ground closure for four games if there was a repeat, and warned that any further problems could result in expulsion from the league. Two weeks later, Newcastle were defeated at home in the play-offs by Sunderland. Newcastle fans began to wreck their own ground and riot inside the stadium. There were a similar number of arrests and police injuries and the riot actually spread onto the pitch. The Football League was benevolent, though, and put it down to Geordie overexuberance. There is an argument that one club has previous form and the other doesn't. However, it's difficult to get a negative record when everyone ignores your transgressions.

To back up my point, on my first visit to St James' Park when I was sixteen, I went up with a friend. A neighbour drove us up there; Barry, an alcoholic who only stopped drinking to get out of the car and smack his dodgy headlight with a screwdriver when it went on the blink. When we got to Newcastle he ditched us outside the Gallowgate End to find a pub, leaving us to make our own way in. So, these two bright-eyed sixteen-year-olds approached a friendly-looking policeman and asked him where the Leeds end could be found. He turned ashen, and at this point I would like to quote him almost verbatim: "Oh Jesus! Thank God you aren't wearing colours. Walk up there, on the other side of the road. Don't talk to anyone, not even each other. You will see your lot at the top." Suitably disturbed, we did as we were told and kept our heads down as hundreds of seemingly menacing Geordie lads strutted past us, obviously hell-bent on our destruction if we dared to look up. We took the police officer's advice, found the bulk of the Leeds fans, and were escorted down the side of the stadium to the seats, where about fifty Leeds fans had bought tickets away from the two thousand or so standing. This was Kevin Keegan's first season and great things were expected of the new messiah, so there was a huge turnout even for this second-round League Cup tie.

Leeds had lost the first leg at Elland Road 1–0, and on this night an early Newcastle goal meant that progression for Newcastle looked like a formality, so we were just hoping to avoid a hammering. The Leeds players had other ideas, though, and this mediocre team decided to save their best performance of the season for our most volatile opponents. Two goals took the game to extra time, then two more in the last two minutes secured an extremely unlikely victory. The two sets of supporters took this in their expected fashion: Leeds fans with barely credible glee and Newcastle fans as if it were the death of a monarch.

As full time approached, I noticed that the Gallowgate End had emptied and assumed that they had trudged off to the city-centre pubs to drown their sorrows. Like Darren at Huddersfield, I was showing my inexperience. As we opened the gate to go out into the streets, we noticed a large group of Newcastle fans waiting for us, and many more ambling past, waiting to see what would happen. Not fancying the odds, we ran back inside and were put in with the Leeds fans in the standing area to be escorted to the train station. Notice the problem here? My friend and I hadn't come by train; we had been driven up by an alcoholic madman. After being escorted to the station, running the gauntlet of abuse and the occasional bottle hurled from a passing bus, we had to make our own way back, at roughly chucking-out time in the pubs. Luckily it wasn't a long walk, but being unfamiliar with the city we got lost and came across a police station with a group of officers stood outside, no doubt waiting for the end of their shift. We knew we'd parked near a monument, so asked one of the friendlier-looking officers the way. Again I would like to quote the conversation:

"You're from Leeds, aren't you?"

"Yeah, but any chance you could keep it between us?"

"Well, you played very well and deserved to win. Find your own fucking monument." He waited until we had gone the same colour as his fellow officer earlier in the evening, then broke into a broad grin. "Only kidding, lads – right around that corner."

We thanked him and walked off in the direction of the car, leaving the officer and his mates giggling like schoolgirls. Barry was waiting for us, still drinking, which he did all the way home. I still wasn't anywhere near as scared as I had been by the thousands of braying, manic Geordies. Four days later the two sides met again in the league at Elland Road. Again it was a vicious affair on the terraces. Kevin Keegan was hit by a ball bearing thrown from the Leeds crowd, and three other players by missiles which could only have come from the Newcastle supporters. Late in the game Newcastle supporters invaded the South Stand and began ripping up seats and throwing them at the Leeds supporters. The punishment? Newcastle fans nothing; Leeds had their standing areas closed for two games. Geordie overexuberance indeed.

But back to the point – throughout the '90s, the '80s sense of injustice became a weary acceptance. Leeds supporters wouldn't have it any other way. We revel in hatred. Hatred is essentially a backhanded compliment: what you hate, you give value to. Why hate something or someone that's worth nothing? This is the Leeds way: hate us if you must, but realise that we love it and it just intensifies our desire. At this time, though, the new younger fans were still coming to terms with the hatred, and it was fantastic to get a result when no one wanted us to.

SWINDON TOWN V LEEDS UNITED, FA CUP FOURTH ROUND, TUESDAY 3RD FEBRUARY 1987

A WARM WELCOME ON A FREEZING DAY

Another tie against lower-league opposition, but only a division lower, and a team riding high within that division. Swindon Town had a formidable home record; Leeds a shocking away record: nine wins, stretching back to the end of 1984 before the Telford game and only three all season, one of them at non-league Telford. The County Ground at Swindon was a tight stadium with the supporters close to the players and a smallish but passionate support. Coupled with the travel distance, the omens were not good. Also, Leeds had never got past the fourth round of the FA Cup, so it was futile to even think about victory.

As was par for the course now, the tie was scheduled for Sunday with a 1.30pm kick-off, meaning a 6am coach from Leeds. The weather became too much for the fixture, though, and it was rescheduled for the following Tuesday evening. Despite the distance for a midweek match and the impending defeat, I travelled to Swindon anyway. I didn't have work the next morning, so what the hell! My reasons have been explained in more detail elsewhere in this book, but can be summarised as another new ground, a day out to appease my overwhelming boredom due to a lack of worthwhile employment, and availability due to said unemployment. With regards to the media position and the FA's stance, Leeds received help from an unusual source. Swindon manager Lou Macari was a former Manchester United player and not someone you would expect to offer help to old rivals. Yet he played the perfect host and welcomed Leeds fans with open arms, hoping that as many as possible could travel. This was a wonderful way to dilute the media bias and they remained pretty much silent throughout the build-up. To be fair, this was hardly a tie to set the pulse racing. The club were taking no risks, however, and the all-ticket restrictions were kept in place, as was the postal application. Even so, I received my ticket and took the coach for the long journey to Wiltshire, I would say more in hope than expectation, but I didn't have much of either, to be honest, and just wanted to visit another ground.

We arrived around two hours before kick-off, and even though the snow had disappeared the cold had not, and I spent a good hour circling the ground just to keep warm. Eventually we were allowed onto the open terrace behind the goal, which was no less cold but at least the proximity of other bodies increased the temperature a little. The game had one of the most one-sided starts I had ever seen. For twenty minutes Swindon slaughtered Leeds. Their fast, physical game was no match for the delicate skills of the likes of Sheridan and Stiles, and Swindon should really have been out of sight by then. All they had for their efforts was a powerful Dave Bamber header that left Mervyn Day with no chance, and Leeds slowly began to find their rhythm. Before the break an own goal put Leeds level, and in the second half a Baird header gave them the tie. Swindon pushed for an equaliser but there were chances for Leeds too, and once Baird scored the result was never really in doubt. This was unchartered territory for Leeds fans, and the not entirely unexpected cries of "Wembley" began to ring around the stadium as Swindon fought in vain to take the tie back to Elland Road. The whistle blew and, after the customary forty-five-minute wait in the stadium for the home fans to clear, we began our five-hour journey home in high spirits.

Despite the fears of the press and the FA, Macari had been correct: the occasion passed with little trouble. However, that didn't stop the press making a meal of the one incident that did occur; one that I witnessed at relatively close hand. When Leeds scored their equaliser towards the end of the first half, there was a punch-up between a couple of supporters in the Leeds end – over, I believe, someone standing on someone else's foot by accident. As happens in these situations, a few friends on either side joined in but it was easily contained and over in less than a minute. Yes, that is exactly how World War I started, but this was a small affair in the annals of football hooliganism and would have been quickly forgotten, except perhaps by the few who were directly involved. This trivial account didn't wash with the tabloid press, though. They had column inches to fill, and commented on how the Leeds equaliser had been the spur for hundreds of Leeds fans to begin fighting amongst themselves. As always in these cases, for the tabloids in particular, the truth matters little. Studying journalism many years later, I was taught that if you need to lie to prove a point then you don't have a point, but our revered red tops must have missed that chapter of the textbook. The Leeds supporters' departing coaches had been bricked by disgruntled Swindon fans, but this had occurred well away from the eyes of the press and would have had little impression on them anyway. With all due respect to their decent team, Swindon is a footballing backwater. Leeds, on the other hand, carry their infamy wherever they go and any story, however contrived, will be believed. This is the main source of contention for Leeds fans. Most would hold up their hands and admit that their fellow supporters have at times behaved like animals and deserved many (although not all) of the punishments handed down to them. Yet other sides' supporters have been equally guilty but allowed to escape punishment. I suppose that, as mentioned earlier, when a bank robber has form the police will come knocking at their door first.

LEEDS UNITED V QUEENS PARK RANGERS, FA CUP FIFTH ROUND, SATURDAY 21ST FEBRUARY 1987

A MEMORABLE DAY AND A CLOSE CALL

The last time Leeds had played in the fifth round of the FA Cup I was still a bright-eyed primary-school student rather than an unemployable layabout gobshite, and Margaret Thatcher was still two years away from starting to impose her own brand of hooliganism on the country, and the north of England in particular.

The team largely regarded, only a few years previously, as the best in Europe managed to go ten years without making any impression on the later rounds of the tournament. In that period, Leeds reached the fourth round three times and only threatened to go further once. In 1983 they took the lead against Arsenal in the last minute of injury time before, in true Leeds style, conceding an equaliser immediately and losing the reply.

The fifth round offered a home tie against First Division Queens Park Rangers, with views about possible progress mixed. Leeds were a division below QPR and since their 1982 relegation had failed to beat top-flight opposition five times in cup competitions. Others pointed to Leeds' decent home form and the fact that QPR, despite having good players, were only a mid-table team. For me it was something I hadn't previously experienced as an adult, and while I suspected that the honest but limited defensive skills of Ormsby and Ashurst would offer little resistance to the attacking prowess of John Byrne and Clive Walker I still carried a small spark of hope. Cup participation at this late stage of the season was new to me and I was determined to enjoy every moment. Yet paradoxically, despite my excitement, I very nearly missed it and the rest of the season, and many to follow.

We need to start that story with my relationship with the younger of my sisters. I am the youngest of the family by thirteen years; the oldest sibling, my only brother, is twenty years older than me. When I was young this sometimes led to my being incredibly spoilt, but also punished excessively for my transgressions as I effectively had five parents. Yes, every year I had a Christmas sack overloaded with presents, but every time I got into trouble they all lined up to administer punishment; think of the passengers queuing up to slap the hysterical woman in the movie *Airplane!* and you get the idea. Anyway, my worst family relationship was with my younger sister, who is thirteen years older than me, and as I grew into my teens and gained a voice we clashed often. We have both mellowed in recent years and now have a much more cordial relationship. In those days, though, we only had to spend about thirty minutes together before we were at each other's throats. An hour together without incident and everyone had had a good day. Usually she would start it, but not all the time, and I was always up for a little antagonism. An offhanded comment about me being a lazy waster would prompt a retort about her brain having a row with her mouth again, and we were off. I remember one Christmas being tempted to buy her a book on do-it-yourself brain surgery. To maintain family harmony, I settled for the obligatory carpet slippers. I suspect the irony would have been totally lost on her anyway. She usually ended any argument by telling me that a spell in the army would do me good; a comment I was pleased to totally ignore. However, after one particularly heated argument when she told me that I didn't have the bottle to join the armed forces, I made the incredibly stupid and naive decision to apply to the Royal Air Force just to prove her wrong. My thinking was thus: apply, fail the aptitude test, and at least I've given it a go, proved her wrong and put in another job application to appease the benefits office.

So I went along to the recruiting office, just off Park Row in central Leeds (I believe it is still there), made a half-arsed attempt at passing the test and then waited around in the city centre for an hour or so while they marked it. I was half tempted to just go home, but a part of me wanted to see whether I was totally stupid or just partially stupid, and by how much I'd failed. After a quick lunch I went back just for interest's sake. You had to state on the form which trade you were looking to join, and you were marked accordingly: a general service candidate would not need as high a score as a pilot or a weapons technician. I'd applied for stores and supplies, which was about halfway up the expected pass grade scale. It was a position of which I had no experience at that time, and one that I'd plucked at random from their glossy brochure when I walked in. I sat back in my chair in the recruiting room, watching other people being called in and witnessing elation and disappointment in equal measure. These people actually *wanted* a career that would send them to distant places to be shot at; I guess we all work in different ways. There seemed to be a fair few who had failed, even for the lesser trades, and although I hadn't found the test that demanding it was clear that I would soon be joining them. If these decent-looking, obviously intelligent people were failing, an uneducated idiot like me had no chance.

"Copley, stores and supplies?" shouted the marking officer, scouring the room for the individual to whom he was set to deliver bad news.

"Yeah, that's me," I said nonchalantly. Time to get out of here and go for a beer; it had been a long morning.

"Passed – go downstairs to the front desk and make an appointment for a medical."

When felt at the same time, fear and astonishment make a potent cocktail. I thought about telling them I was a Leeds fan to make them reconsider their decision; it had always worked previously. I even thought about demanding a recount. In the end I just went downstairs in a state of shock and arranged the medical for a few days later, which proved to be straightforward.

The next step was to go back to the RAF office to fill in some paperwork. Now, as I say, football violence had left me indifferent unless it was up close. I remember the fear of being confronted by Bradford fans outside Odsal, I remember fearing for my life after being chased out of Kirkstall Fair by baseball-bat-wielding thugs, I remember the fear of feral police dogs and panicking horses at many away grounds. Nothing, though, had prepared me for the abject terror of having a booklet placed in front of me with 'OFFICIAL APPLICATION FOR SERVICE' printed on the cover. How the hell had it come to this? Why couldn't I just tell my sister I was the lazy, pitiful coward she thought me and admit defeat? Then I thought, *I'm here, there's no way they'll accept me anyway, so let's just fill it in for the fun, then I've taken it as far as I can. They can fail me, but I've come all this way and at least I tried.* I knew it wouldn't go further, so I filled in the form with my disgraceful, totally illegible handwriting. One look at it and they would surely decline to even interview me.

A week later I was sat in front of the commanding officer, having already passed an interview with a sergeant. I hoped he couldn't see me shaking and failed to register the quiver in my voice. I'd forgotten all about Leeds United and the cup run and was focused on saving my own petrified butt and retaining my personal mantra of 'Cowardice is the better part of valour.' As the interview went on I grew more and more fearful. Telling him I was a Leeds United supporter had no detrimental effect; in fact it appeared to work in my favour – experience of unarmed combat, maybe? It seemed that the interview was going unexpectedly well. In fact, it was going disastrously well, if you can forgive the oxymoron. The commander finished the interview and asked me to step outside for a few minutes while he considered his decision, the agony of which was comparable with waiting for the final whistle when you're winning a vital game, with the added problem that a last-minute equaliser wasn't likely to shape the rest of my life. He called me back in and I tried to convince myself that this was what I wanted. I'd probably be able to see the fifth-round game anyway, which would end in defeat so I wouldn't miss a cup run. It was a good career on offer, and there was a remote chance that when I got home in five years or so Leeds would be back in the top flight. This was all nonsense, of course; I was about to join the armed forces and, mortified by my stupidity, I sat there waiting for him to speak, wondering if I was allowed a last request.

He took off his glasses and stared at me evenly. "You put yourself across well, but I don't think you are quite ready yet; you lack a little maturity, if I'm honest. Come back in a year – we'll have to give you another medical, but we'll process you straight through from there."

Had I been standing I would probably have passed out; such was my relief. I thanked him and promised faithfully that I would be back in twelve months. For those of you reading this who struggle with the concept of irony – err, yeah, right! My curiosity got the better of me, though, and I had to ask what the next step would have been, had I been successful.

"Oh, you'd be on a train to RAF Scampton in Lincolnshire for six weeks of basic training first thing Monday morning," he said with a knowing smile. There is a possibility he was lying; I doubt it would have happened that quickly. He knew a chancer when he saw one.

It was Thursday, still nine days before the QPR game. Instead of watching my team run out in the fifth round for the first time in ten years I would probably have been attempting (and failing) to scale a twelve-foot wall on a mud-splattered assault course while a disgusted drill sergeant screamed at me to pull my finger out. It occurred to me that the near marine experience I believed I'd encountered training at Farsley Celtic was a mere stroll in the park

I've contemplated many times since how my life would have turned out had I been accepted by the RAF, but I'm convinced I wouldn't have made it. I have neither the bravery, the common sense nor, admittedly, the sense of duty to be a serviceman. I had always been someone who questions everything, not nothing. Still, there was a tinge of regret as I had at least prepared properly and done my research. They sold the job very well and a small part of me had hoped to be accepted. My inner coward and manic obsessive won the day, though. Nonetheless, the whole episode did work in my favour. My sister and the rest of the family started to show me some begrudging respect and backed off a little, and incredibly I haven't failed an interview since. Time to put the opportunity of a lifetime behind me and get on with my pitiful existence. I understand that many are intoxicated by a career change and the 'see the world' lifestyle but I had an FA Cup fifth-round tie to think about and I was starting to panic a little on that front.

There was certainly a renewed optimism around the city and many people who had shown little interest over the past few seasons suddenly craved tickets. There proved to be no need for tickets, however, as the club decided not to make the game all ticket and estimated a crowd of twenty-three thousand. On face value, this was a reasonable assumption and a sensible decision. Only two games – league leaders Portsmouth and the Boxing Day game against Sunderland – had attracted crowds of over twenty thousand and the Sunderland crowd had been swelled by a sizeable away following. QPR would not bring such numbers, and with Leeds struggling to keep up with the play-off places in the division the game wasn't expected to be a big crowd-puller.

However, this was the FA Cup, British football's showpiece, and the Leeds board grossly underestimated the city's interest in the event. Walking to the ground, it was clear that this was going to be no ordinary game, and those of us who attended every game noticed a huge increase in the number of people at the turnstiles. Whilst it was true that there weren't a great deal more supporters in the expensive seats, the standing areas were packed to capacity and, portentously in light of what happened at Hillsborough two years later, possibly beyond. Over thirty-one thousand packed into the ground; the highest attendance since a home game with European Champions Liverpool in 1982.

Arriving twenty minutes before kick-off, I realised that it was going to be impossible to get to my usual spot in The Kop – top half, centre left – and had to settle for a spot close to the top and further out to the left. There was a noise inside the stadium that had not been witnessed by us seasoned veterans in many a year, and the standing areas were bouncing. The players seemed to take heart from this and from the start attacked QPR with fast, direct football. QPR's pretty, space-age game was no match for Leeds' high intensity and the home team were soon in the lead, frequent scorer Ian Baird, with his usual willingness to put his head where others would think twice about putting their feet, heading home at the far post. Leeds continued to dominate the first half but there were no further goals then. The half-time period was spent in a carnival atmosphere that Elland Road had not seen for years certainly not in my time. Normality was restored early in the second half, though, when Leeds midfielder David Rennie, for reasons best known to himself, decided to give Mervyn Day some shooting practice and directed a well-placed curling shot beyond his own goalkeeper. Day looked totally bemused by Rennie's contribution to the QPR cause, and was probably taken by surprise since no one on the QPR side had shown any such endeavour. The situation was so stereotypically Leeds, as was the fighting amongst a few dozen fans in the Lowfields standing area immediately after the goal; an incident which was on this occasion overlooked by the national press even though they would have been justified in reporting it. Amongst the jubilation the local press did, however, find column space to cover the trouble, complete with a photo of a smiling, bloodied youth being escorted away by a police officer. On this occasion, I found the conflict totally perplexing. I wasn't in the stand so had no idea what sparked it, but Leeds fans fighting amongst themselves in such numbers was unheard of even given our violent element. There had been occasional scrapes at the back of the Kop End between the left and right sides of the terrace – yes, we could be *that* territorial and petty – but nothing on this scale. It seemed to go on for a few minutes in the end pen of the terrace and the police struggled to contain the trouble. I refuse to believe that the cause was something as simple as someone stepping on someone else's foot, as was the case at Swindon. The supporters involved also showed no interest in attacking the thousand or so QPR fans present. The scrap was contained in a small section; close to the away fans, but partitioned off well. I'd never really seen the point in deliberately bringing the club into disrepute, but at least I understood the notions of territory and partisanship. There was none of that here, though; just a bizarre adverse reaction to an averagely talented midfielder momentarily forgetting in which direction his team was playing. Maybe it's best not to inquire about such things.

Around the rest of the stadium there was simply an air of resignation; we knew the script from now on. QPR would smell blood, Leeds would defend desperately, and QPR would get a late winner. The Leeds players, however, were blissfully unaware of this set outcome and continued to force QPR back and create chances. The supporters were buoyant again and the noise increased. With five minutes to go, dreamland beckoned. Sheridan sent in a near post corner, newly signed striker John Pearson flicked it on, and captain Brendon Ormsby gave it a powerful head home in front of the Kop End. Wild celebrations ensued and the noise was deafening. This was an odd ending. No shrieking from the supporters in response to the whistle; just a wild party. It was assumed that QPR wouldn't score if they played until Tuesday, and they showed no inclination to prove us wrong. For my part it was a bit bewildering. I obviously took part in the celebrations, but the pace of the game in the second half had consumed me completely, to the point where, when Ormsby scored, I'd assumed there was a good fifteen minutes left. When the final whistle came I'd thought it was for a free kick and wondered why the Leeds fans were bouncing around like Zebedee on acid simply for gaining an offside decision. It was only when the players themselves came to us to join in the celebration that I realised it was actually over. For the first time in ten years I was going to watch the latter rounds of the tournament with a vested interest rather than a dismal yearning.

I went into town that night to celebrate and the place was rocking. I did my favourite tour of Harlequin's, Jacomelli's, Oscar's, The Bond, Stumps and finally The Bank on Park Row, celebrating with people I didn't know and have never seen since. It must have been giro week because I usually just stayed in Harlequin's with its offer of fifty pence a pint rather than taking on a pub crawl. I remained in The Bank until closing time, then left with a few like-minded fellows and a friend who didn't really share my excitement but humoured me anyway. We all burst onto the streets, screaming about Wembley. In the excitement I'd forgotten to save enough money for a taxi, but not to worry; I floated the five miles back to Rodley on a wave of unbridled optimism. I suspect my friend had enough money for his half of the taxi fare, but felt duty-bound to stay with me and found the walk a little more of a chore.

Success is relative and all down to scale. Maybe fans of hugely successful clubs would treat an FA Cup fifth-round win as just another game, but this was a virgin experience for the new wave of young Leeds fans brought up on disillusionment and despair. Cup fever now gripped the city in a way it hadn't since the '70s.

WIGAN ATHLETIC V LEEDS UNITED, FA CUP SIXTH ROUND, SUNDAY 15TH MARCH 1987

ANOTHER BLOODY SUNDAY, AND FA INTERFERENCE

It seems almost paradoxical to mention Leeds United and the FA Cup sixth round in the same sentence. In later years this would prove to be even more the case. Up to 2021, Leeds reached the sixth round only three more times, twice going out to lower-league opposition at that stage. This would explain the renewed optimism. In the early rounds it's just a case of enjoying the refreshing change of a knockout competition and seeing how far you can progress. When you get to the quarter-final you started dreaming of the famous Twin Towers and really begin to hope. Only eight teams are left at this stage and, in 1987's competition, Manchester United, Liverpool and Everton, renowned cup teams, were already out. The draw was beginning to open up and hopes were high. Six First Division teams, one Second Division and one Third Division were left. Everyone from the top flight obviously wanted to play one of the lesser teams: Leeds from the Second Division or Wigan Athletic from the Third. The draw was kind to the lower teams, though, and they were drawn together, with Wigan at home. This was a great opportunity for Leeds, although they would have preferred a home tie. Still, it was a chance to progress and the city was buzzing. It was not straightforward, though. Wigan were towards the top of the Third Division, with an excellent home record and unbeaten since November; a run of nineteen games. They had also knocked out First Division Norwich City at home and hammered Second Division Hull City in the last round. This was a great opportunity for them too. Add to this the fact that Baird and Ormsby, Leeds' only scorers in the competition, were both suspended and the gap of one division became a real leveller. Few were brave enough to predict the outcome with any real belief.

That last piece of information highlights the relationship Leeds United had (and still have) with the football authorities. Every Leeds supporter will tell you that the FA, the Football League and even UEFA have always had it in for them. Opposition supporters put this down to paranoia, and the truth probably lies somewhere in between. The borderline hysteria of the competition's earlier rounds tends to support the Leeds view a little bit, and the suspensions of Baird and Ormsby betrayed the authorities' less-than-humanitarian side. Both players were suspended for one game. As Leeds looked to be floundering in the league a little, the club decided to bring forward a previously postponed league game against Portsmouth to the Wednesday before the Wigan game. This would mean that Ormsby and Baird would be suspended for that game and therefore free to play against Wigan in the cup. This again shows the value placed on the FA Cup at that time, as Leeds were not out of contention for a play-off place and a game at promotion-chasing Portsmouth would provide an opportunity to pick up valuable points with a full-strength team. Yet Leeds placed more importance on the cup and used the Portsmouth game for the captain and leading scorer to serve out their suspensions. The FA didn't like that though. They decided that, as the booking offences had been committed in an FA Cup tie, the suspensions should also be served in one, and decreed that Ormsby and Baird would still be suspended for the Wigan quarter-final even if neither had played at Portsmouth. I'm not sure if this had ever been done before, but as paranoid Leeds fans we took it very personally, and saw it as another excuse to undermine our efforts. Leeds gained a creditable 1-1 draw at Portsmouth with Baird and Ormsby in the team, but it left Leeds in a vulnerable position for the cup game, playing an inform team who had an excellent home record and (as the underdogs) the support of the nation, without their captain and leading scorer (and only goalscorers in the competition). Just because you are paranoid, it doesn't mean they are not out to get you.

With this in mind, I wasn't hopeful. Everything was set up for a giant killing to enhance the romance of the cup, and the Yorkshire Hun would be slayed by the plucky small team from across the Pennines who had only been a league side for the past eight years. Leeds were always primed for a giant killing. In recent years, they had lost to Scunthorpe, Peterborough, Chester (sitting at the bottom of the Fourth Division at the time), Huddersfield Town and Oxford, and been held by Walsall. Even the 'Super Leeds' of the previous decade had not been immune to a giant killing. Chester City, Colchester United, Sunderland, Bristol City and, a little later, Notts County and Crystal Palace all defeated Leeds from the lower leagues, and Leeds famously took two games to get past non-league Wimbledon.

While there was optimism it was tinged with realism and, for many, a sense of foreboding. Despite this, everyone wanted to see the game. Only two thousand tickets were available for away fans and these soon sold out. However, Leeds City Council showed some initiative for once – or saw the chance to earn a quick quid; draw your own conclusion – and decided to screen beam-back live coverage of the game in the Town Hall and Queens Hall, to give supporters who didn't have tickets a chance to see it. This also encouraged Leeds fans not to travel to Wigan. This was the only cup tie I didn't attend – the tickets went to supporters who'd seen more away games than I – so I took my place at the Queens Hall with about six thousand others.

It was an odd experience in many ways. The quality of beam-back coverage wasn't great in those days; it was like watching the game through a thin haze. It was also a little strange screaming encouragement at people who were fifty miles away with no hope of hearing you. At that time I had seen Leeds live on TV only once since the 1975 European Cup final. That had been for a third-round FA Cup tie against Everton in 1985, and had provided very little to shout about. I don't need to tell you the result: it was an FA Cup tie. As in the Stoke game earlier in the season, shouting at a TV screen as opposed to the radio helped ease my sense of helplessness. The game has changed now and TV consumption has come to matter just as much as live consumption. We all find different ways to follow our obsession, and although the diehards look down smugly on the armchair fans, it's hard to argue that they don't have their place. With attendance prices now out of the budget of many supporters, TV holds an important place in following football. Living in China, I understand this more than ever. Proxy servers allow me to watch every game; something that wasn't possible thirty years ago. In fact, I feel it would have been very difficult to even find the results while living in post-Mao China. But without any live games apart from the FA Cup final, in the '80s live consumption was everything, and this was one of the first uses of beam-back footage. Football supporters are a versatile bunch, though, and once the place filled up the atmosphere became raucous – no doubt fuelled by alcohol, but never likely to spill over into violence without the attendance of rival supporters.

The game played out in predictable fashion. Wigan came at Leeds early on and created a few half-chances, then Leeds grew into the game and created a few of their own. It was a tense affair, though, and not one for the purist. No score at half-time, and not much to suggest a breakthrough from either side. A replay at Elland Road looked likely and would have suited most of us. The second half turned on a couple of incidents; one at each end. Wigan's Northern Irish striker Bobby Campbell, who had put away a harder chance against Leeds for Bradford City earlier in the season, headed against the post with the goal gaping and Mervyn Day well beaten. Within a few minutes, at the other end a clearance fell to Leeds' John Stiles – son of World Cup winner Nobby – who produced a cool finish from twenty yards to beat Wigan goalkeeper Roy Tunks. Stiles was a bit-part player – a lower-division John Sheridan, if you like – and an unlikely hero. He probably wouldn't have been playing if new signing Mark Aizlewood hadn't been cup-tied. Even so, a goal is a goal, and the explosion of relief wasn't in any way diminished because of the identity of the scorer. A few more minutes passed and, to more astonishment, left back Micky Adams cut in from the left, swung his right foot at the ball from twenty-five yards, and was as surprised as anyone to see his effort nestle in the top corner. Relief turned to unadulterated joy and the last ten minutes were a wild celebration. Strangers hugged each other; normally reticent supporters screamed themselves hoarse as six thousand jubilant yet incredulous supporters screamed, "Wembley's on a Sunday." This was a rather sardonic reference to Leeds' every away cup tie, and many away league games, being switched to a Sunday. The authorities obviously believed that the lack of access to alcohol and the observance of the Lord's day would deter mindless violence.

The day of the game was immaterial, though. The team whom everyone wanted to be thrown out of the competition in the third round were now one game away from English football's showcase finale, thanks to goals from a bit-part player who was to play fewer than twenty more games for the club, and a newly signed left back hitting one with his swinger. As with the other two ties against lower-league opposition, Wigan probably deserved a draw. But luck was with the Devil incarnate that year, and the team everyone hated had a chance to gatecrash the end-of-season party. The rest of England looked on in dismay, and the FA shifted uncomfortably in their ivory tower, wondering how they were going to get out of this one.

COVENTRY CITY V LEEDS UNITED, FA CUP SEMI-FINAL, SUNDAY 12TH APRIL 1987

WHAT MIGHT HAVE BEEN: PRESENT AND FUTURE

Meaningful games past the end of March were something of a rarity for Leeds fans. Mediocrity dictated that the team was just about competent enough to avoid being dragged into a relegation dogfight but nowhere near good enough to fight for the major prizes. Leeds had reasons to regard the end of the season with more than passing interest on just four occasions between 1976 and 1990, apart from this one. There had been a successful campaign to secure a UEFA Cup place in 1979 and an unsuccessful fight against relegation in 1982. The other times were during the wilderness years of the Second Division, with Leeds only threatening to get out of it on two occasions. In 1985 they needed to win on the final day at already promoted Birmingham City and hope that Manchester City, Portsmouth, Brighton and Blackburn all failed to do so. As we've come to expect, Leeds lost and all the others won, which resulted in the riot at St Andrew's stadium. Sometimes you get the supporters and the luck that you deserve. The final time was the previously mentioned last home game in 1986, when Leeds looked like leaving the division in a totally different direction to the one they craved.

So April 1987 was an exciting time to be a Leeds fan. The cup run had also resulted in an upturn in league form and now Leeds were firmly in contention for a play-off place too. However, this was still the back end of the golden age of the FA Cup and the city was gripped by the fever. I believe the saying is 'starve a fever', and Leeds United had certainly been starved of cup success in the preceding ten years.

The four teams left in the semi-final were Leeds, Tottenham Hotspur, Coventry City and Watford. Of those, on third-round day you would have placed money on Tottenham alone being in the last four; the rest would have been way down the list. It's stating the obvious to say that Leeds would have preferred to avoid Tottenham, and our acute paranoia suspected that the FA was busting a gut to pair us with them. This would have left them with a problem, though. Leeds and Tottenham fans had recent history, and unfinished business as far as the Leeds fans were concerned. The last time Leeds were in the top flight, a young Leeds fan had been killed outside White Hart Lane and his comrades had sworn vengeance ever since. Pairing the two at a neutral venue, allowing for twenty-odd thousand of each set of supporters flooding to an unfamiliar stadium, was a recipe for disaster, so the two were kept apart. Deliberately? Draw your own conclusions.

As it was, Leeds were to face Coventry City. Coventry were perennial top-flight strugglers who always seemed to find a way to survive. Despite being in constant relegation trouble they had been in the top division since 1968 and were the fourth longest-surviving top-flight side behind Arsenal, Everton and Liverpool. They held this record until in 2001 the inevitable finally came and they were relegated. This Coventry team were different, though, and could quite easily be recognised as the best Coventry side ever. They were in the top half of the division all season and had beaten Tottenham and future league champions Everton at home. In the cup they had beaten Manchester United and a half-decent

Sheffield Wednesday team, and won away at Stoke in the fifth round. As the same Stoke team had demolished Leeds 7–2 just four months earlier, grounds for optimism were few. Yet we chose to ignore this and believe that anything was possible.

Hillsborough, home of Sheffield Wednesday and the venue for Coventry's quarter-final win, was chosen as the venue. Talking on his show, *Saint and Greavsie*, former Tottenham legend Jimmy Greaves, for reasons known only to himself, stated that the choice of venue was a victory for the hooligans of Leeds. It would seem that the arduous task of travelling seventy-five miles as opposed to thirty-five would have proved too much for a team of First Division professionals and the extra forty minutes in a team bus would provide an unfair advantage to a just-above-mid-table Second Division team. In the meantime, the Leeds hooligan following would be energised by an extra hour in bed and ready to cause havoc that would be beyond them if they'd had the exhausting task of travelling another hour or so to, say, Villa Park and having to change trains at Manchester. Even so, the nation seemed to agree with Greaves and few neutrals were looking for a United win.

Here we have the enigma that is Leeds United. The British love an underdog; partly due to our 'jack of all trades, master of none' attitude to sport, but also probably deriving from the Blitz and Dunkirk backs-to-the-wall spirit. To be fair, I totally concur with this attitude and love to see Billy Big Balls taken to the cleaners by a relative nobody. However, as previously mentioned, even in their heyday (and definitely more recently) Leeds had had their fair share of lower-league humiliation and this was their chance to turn the tables. Due to the relative league standings they were very much the underdogs in this game, yet the entire nation seemed to be itching for Coventry to succeed. There are other reasons for this: as a recently successful side, Leeds had had their moments and Coventry had had none, so in a way it was gratifying to see a team used to struggling actually having some success. I suppose if we are taking history into account, Coventry were the underdogs no matter how much better their team actually was. It's still hard to qualify, though, and to imagine any team other than Leeds being regarded as the goliath on such an occasion. Nevertheless, Leeds fans had begun to revel in animosity and actually welcomed the 'ogre' tag. There was even a chance of success: a tie against the stars of Tottenham would have been regarded as an unwinnable game and treated as a day out, with a plucky performance being a decent result. Coventry, however, were a good team but beatable. Teams hovering around mid-table were always prone to an off day and Coventry were not much better than QPR. So there was a chance – a slim one, but still a chance.

One of the quirks of this tie – and one of the prime problems involved in the Hillsborough Disaster exactly two years later – was the respective levels of support. Despite being a division lower, Leeds' average gate was almost double that of Coventry. Obviously it would have made sense for Leeds to have the majority of the tickets. However, South Yorkshire Police and the FA were much more concerned with geography than with the actual people attending the event. The ground was situated so that Coventry fans approaching from the south would arrive at Wednesday's huge Spion Kop, whilst Leeds fans coming from the north would enter the smaller and soon to be infamous Leppings Lane End. Allowing for each team to be allotted one of the seated stands to either side of the pitch, this meant that Coventry City (average gate: around twelve thousand) would be allocated twenty-eight thousand tickets and Leeds United (average gate: nineteen thousand) would get twenty-two thousand. Naturally uproar ensued, but Leeds' claims to more tickets were completely ignored and the allocations stood. Many Leeds fans who wouldn't be able to get tickets decided to try their luck at Coventry, with the Midlands club making the sensible decision to send back five hundred tickets for fear of them falling into the wrong hands. So, all the Coventry supporters who wanted a ticket for the biggest game in their history got one, and rightly so. It's refreshing to see supporters for the big games all getting to see their team; especially supporters who had known little more than yearly struggle. I just wish it could have been for any other game and under different circumstances.

Things went rather differently at Elland Road, though: after season ticket holders and supporters' club members had had first refusal, there were a mere six thousand tickets remaining of the twenty-two thousand to be put on general sale. These were due to go on sale on a Thursday morning at 10am. What happened at Elland Road that morning will never be forgotten by those who attended. Aware of the possibility of a well oversubscribed sell-out, I and three friends decided to set off early for the ground. (Although I had my ticket, I was queuing for a friend who couldn't get a day off work and was willing to pay me handsomely for taking his place in the queue.) So early, in fact, that we got a taxi at 3am, some seven hours before the tickets were due to go on sale. The incredulous driver got us there in twenty minutes, expecting, much as we did, to find a deserted stadium and drop us at the front of the queue.

When the taxi pulled up at 3.20 there were at least five hundred people already taking part in that quaint English tradition of queuing. Some had been there since 7pm the previous evening. This was going to be no ordinary day. We joined the back of the queue and a steady stream of people formed behind us. Given the possibility of being oversubscribed, and having to endure a six-hour wait, the atmosphere was tense. There had already been fighting between queue-jumpers around midnight and there was lots of pushing and shoving to maintain a spot. By 6am the event could easily have been mistaken for a home game and the noise and atmosphere around the ground were almost palpable. Around 7am the crowd at the perimeter of the stadium was so great that the gate into the concourse was opened to allow a few hundred early arrivals to wait outside the ticket office, which at that time was situated outside the West Stand close to the players' entrance. Such was the eagerness of the mass of people to maintain their position that a young Leeds fan was pushed over and knocked unconscious. A couple of concerned supporters crouched beside him, showing distracted concern whilst also uttering expletives to those passing by or accidentally stepping over him. If I were to give this story a decent narrative, I would tell you that my conscience stopped me in my tracks and I paused to check that the lad was OK. A further twist would see me sending him my ticket, overcome by guilt. Neither of these things happened. I was a trifle surprised by the prostrate figure below me but, despite mild concern, continued to follow the hordes to the ticket office. The boy recovered and did receive an anonymous free ticket, but not from me. My selfishness dictates that a romantic narrative can only stretch so far. Soon after 10am I got the ticket and, as soon as I passed through the gate, was offered five times its face value. The crowd circled the entire stadium and continued down Elland Road towards the ring road, finally starting to thin out by the bridge just past the training ground. No one who turned up after 7am got a ticket, and twenty-two thousand supporters – enough to take up Leeds' entire allocation – went to Elland Road in an attempt to do so. Thirty-eight thousand people in total made a physical attempt to get tickets. Add in those fans who would have purchased one had they not pre-empted the problems and I think it's safe to say that Leeds could have filled the stadium. Coventry, on the other hand, failed to sell their allocation of just over fifty-five per cent of the tickets. Liverpool were to suffer equal if not greater difficulties – in exactly the same way, at the same event at the same stadium – two years later. They were the most successful club of the era, and demand for tickets would have been much higher.

The problems encountered two years later also highlighted strategies that were put in place for the Leeds game but not enforced in 1989. One of those came from Leeds themselves: a park-and-ride system in which service buses from Leeds ferried supporters to Sheffield for the game. The system had been hugely successful at the Wigan game and therefore was used again. Another thing in place was ticket checks. Everyone arriving by bus, car or train was checked, and anyone without a ticket was turned away. Four of us arrived by car and were at Hillsborough by 9.30, two and a half hours before kick-off. Even at this early stage, there were plenty of police around and we were asked to show our tickets three times before we even got to the stadium. Looking at the layout of the Leppings Lane End it is easy to see why Liverpool supporters were drawn towards the central pens: the signposting was poor and, in the middle section, seemed to indicate that they were the only option. Remember, to many supporters this would have been an unfamiliar stadium.

We were lucky in that we approached from the other side and encountered the left-side outer pen first. There we entered and there we stayed, towards the back of pen five, for the duration of the game. To start with, the stand was almost empty and we had a clear view. I have to say, though, that by kick-off time I'd lost the people I was with and, despite standing six feet tall, was unable to see most of the nearside goal. Only its top two feet were visible to me. This was something I'd never encountered before in over one hundred games. It was also almost impossible to jump up to see the rest of the goal due to the number of people packed in around me. I heard that people in pens three and four suffered even more and there were numerous minor injuries. For us in the outer pen, it was uncomfortable but not unbearable. It was packed as full as I've ever seen a stand, though, and I would certainly say that there was no room for even one more human being. When I watch documentaries about Hillsborough and see that pens three and four contained double the recommended number of people, I think back to that hot, stifling day in April and try to imagine doubling that already intense crush of bodies. I also think about my chances of getting out. I was a fit twenty-year-old, but so were many of the Liverpool fans who perished that day. Survival of the fittest was no real factor; it was sheer dumb luck. Add in my occasional breathing problems (which developed into asthma some years later) and I fear my chances would have been minimal.

Liverpool's opponents that day were Nottingham Forest. The same geographical equations came into effect. In an earlier round Forest had been fortunate to knock out Leeds at the City Ground; a game I attended. It's unlikely but not a huge stretch of the imagination to conceive of Leeds winning that game and being Liverpool's opponents in the semi-final. The logistics would have been different and Leeds would almost certainly have been given the Leppings Lane End. Would we have been subjected to ticket checks that Liverpool fans weren't? Maybe not; our reputation for mindless violence had died down by then, as had football hooliganism in most of the country. Would I have been at the game? There is no way I would have missed it, considering how much the FA Cup and my team meant to me. Would I have headed for the central pens? There are no certainties, but I can't rule it out; there were occasions when I watched games from those areas. It's down to logistics on the day. Would the same sequence of events have played out? Same answer as above. Would I have survived being in the wrong place at the wrong time? I have serious doubts. There are too many variables involved to make a real objective judgement but I feel it would simply have been down to fortune.

Like any football fan, I remember where I was when Hillsborough occurred. I was at yet another meaningless end-of-season game against Brighton & Hove Albion at Elland Road. News started to filter through that the game at Hillsborough had not kicked off, and with the usual casual indifference, people assumed it was due to crowd trouble. Even though aggression at matches had been dying down for a couple of years, there was still an omnipresent threat. Yes, things had been changing, but the menace was always apparent and any setback came as little surprise. Later, as people made their way home, the truth became apparent: the radios of cars waiting in static traffic queues told supporters walking past of at least fifty dead. There was huge sadness but, amazingly, no real sense of shock. Heysel and Bradford were still fresh in the memory and, whilst it would be unfair to say that the average supporter had become desensitised, it was apparent that few lessons had been learned by the authorities and another disaster was always a possibility. Those of us with any sense of perspective recognised a watershed moment when we saw one, and I'm sure that many of the Leeds fans walking silently and sombrely up Lowfields Road that day remembered being in that exact place exactly two years earlier and reflected on their own good fortune.

For me there were other, stronger memories. The date – the 15th April – will of course stay with football fans, and especially Liverpool fans, forever. For me, though, there is another crucial date. A little over a week later, on the 23rd April, my girlfriend told me that she was pregnant with my first child. She had known for a few weeks but had been fearful of telling me, wary of my possible reaction. That day she told me and, due to that more pressing personal matter, Hillsborough was pushed from my mind.

I still think about that day, though, and on the anniversary, wherever I am, whatever I'm doing, I take part in a minute's silence. I think about the unfortunates who died. I think about their abject terror: gasping for breath, having the life sucked out of them. I think about them pleading for help from others around them who were in the same desperate state; unable to help themselves, never mind others. The sheer helplessness must have compounded the terror as they could see no way out. I think about their despair at police officers showing complete indifference to their safety. I think about their lives and their families and how everyone around them was affected by the tragedy; the stories of mental breakdowns and suicides among those unable to process the disaster. I think about their anger and humiliation as the police, aided by the press and the government, shamefully attempted to shift the blame onto those most afflicted.

Incredibly, for a long time, those involved did this with relative success. The officers assumed – as did we, thirty miles away – that it was crowd trouble. They weren't thirty miles away, though; they weren't even thirty feet away, and they were paid and trained to protect people and react to such situations. How could they not recognise what was happening in front of them? There is a huge difference between bellowing in anger and screaming in fear; they must have come across both in their experiences with both aggressors and victims. Yet there they were, acting with either ignorance or indifference to a devastating tragedy unfolding before their eyes. This is, of course, another face of the same casual indifference with which we supporters had come to regard hooliganism, yet at Hillsborough it was the untrained supporters who reacted quickest. Liverpool fans pulled others into the stand above and over the fence, as well as using advertising hoardings as makeshift stretchers while trained officers watched them, unsure how to react. Some, astonishingly, can be seen trying to push supporters back into the crush.

It is of course unfair to tarnish all officers in this way: the video footage shows that there were many who reacted quickly and did everything they could to help. Their superiors, though, acted with breathtaking arrogance and callous indifference as they immediately instigated an elaborate cover-up based almost entirely on lies and subterfuge. Apportioning blame to the victims of the disaster was contemptible in the extreme and I've always felt that this was a pivotal moment for the police; the moment they lost the public's respect and trust. They underestimated the determination of Liverpool's people to expose the lies and finally get to the truth, and it's easy to see the factors that drove the survivors to get justice for their loved ones. The treatment of the families in the aftermath of the disaster was staggering.

In the defence of the officers on the ground, they are taught to accept orders from above unconditionally; there is little room for personal interpretation. The problem was that they were getting no leadership from above and were left in a position where they had to think on their feet in a crisis situation. Many acted admirably, even heroically; some froze, and who amongst us can say with any certainty that we wouldn't have done the same? Others, of course, just saw a baying mob and ignored those pleading for their lives, believing all fans to be the same. They are best left with their conscience.

It was left to the supporters to act first and try to stop an impending disaster, which they attempted with incredible perception in the beginning and tragic heroism later as the disaster unfolded. How many got clear of the crush and then, after catching their breath, rushed straight back to help others? All of this occurred in the presence of trained police officers waiting patiently for orders from above that never came as their superiors were either standing frozen in the headlights or busy composing their cover stories. As attitudes towards the police changed I feel there was also a softening of prejudice towards football fans. A nation watched as perceived hardened criminals did the police's job for them and attempted to save the trapped and dying, sometimes putting their own lives at risk in the process.

It has to be said, as well, that football supporters of the time have to shoulder some responsibility for Hillsborough too. The fences that killed those poor people were there as a result of the behaviour of certain fans whom we had come to regard almost as an accepted part of the game. Many of us had not been directly involved in the sickening violence of the previous years but most of us had revelled in the infamy it created. Who can say that they never felt a touch of pride at being part of a huge police escort in a neighbouring town, pounding out their war cry as nervous locals looked on or dragged their children across the street? It's easy to blame the police alone, but there were many other variables involved. Rundown stadiums; penny-pinching directors; arrogant FA officials; lazy, stereotyping media; and bellicose fans all played a part in a disaster that had been inevitable for years. A similar disaster in the '70s at Ibrox, home of Glasgow Rangers, and numerous near misses had been overlooked and the portents ignored. The shameless cover-up by the police which was eventually laid bare showed the top-level arrogance involved across the UK, and they should absolutely face justice, if not for manslaughter or murder then most definitely on conspiracy charges. Yet there is a collective responsibility too. We fans have to take some responsibility, if not for our direct involvement, then for our casual indifference which allowed this disease to fester for so long. I can't speak for other supporters, but neither can I help feeling partly responsible, and maybe this is why my antagonism towards incompetent policing is so vitriolic.

Then I can't help thinking about how easily it could have been me. How, with just a twist of fate and a couple of positive results, I could have been in those pens that day, as I was two years prior to the disaster. I consider how unlikely it is that I would have been able to survive in such circumstances, given my breathing problems. Then my mind switches to my family and their reactions, and especially my girlfriend, carrying my unborn child; a child she was too scared to tell me about, a child who would never know his father, simply due to a chain of catastrophic events and, it has to be said, gross negligence and incompetence which have still to be accounted for properly after all these years. I don't want to make this sickening tragedy about me and it is selfish to do so. But when the situation is real and the chain of events so random and difficult to determine, it's hard not to feel that you got lucky. I cannot watch a Hillsborough documentary without shedding a tear; in fact, many tears. I shed them for the victims, of course, and their families whose grief is real, raw and permanent. I feel I have no real right to shed tears for something that is not personal to me; where I don't know anyone involved. I do, however, experience resonance and empathy. As football supporters, despite the rivalries, we are a huge family and we feel the same pain, suffer the same anguish, and vent about the same frustrations over crowd safety, police negligence and public hostility. We empathise because we are, essentially, part of the same club. Those who had been to Hillsborough knew instinctively, without being told, where the problem in the stadium was; we had personal experience from two years before and there had been other problems in the Leppings Lane End in the past. So we'd suffered a similar experience but to a much lesser extent, and that meant that we could see how easily it could happen. Therefore, shedding a few tears for people who suffered horrors that resonate so readily is understandable. But I shed them for myself too: for what might have happened and how the dynamic of my entire family would have changed. I think of my son growing up without ever knowing his father. I realise that my second son would never have been born. I grieve for what might have been as well as what actually happened. Then I really feel guilty, because the experience is not mine to grieve for. I have no right to grieve over a situation that I wasn't part of; from which I suffered no loss. Then I grieve yet again over the whole shambolic process.

THE GAME

Despite the romance of this wonderful tournament and the excellent football it offers, FA Cup semi-finals are usually tense, low-scoring affairs. With odd exceptions, the teams are very tightly matched and, thinking of the prize that awaits them, tense and less likely to play some free-flowing football. During the commentary for this game, former Manchester United manager Ron Atkinson described the semi-finals as wars of attrition and that is perfectly apt: teams and individuals are afraid of making mistakes and as a result the games are quite defensive and often dull. This is, of course, a neutral point of view; those with a vested interest would no doubt view even the dourest semi-final as an all-action, energy-sapping event worthy of being branded a purist's fantasy. But on the outside, everything is too cagey, and there is too much at stake. Often semi-finals are decided by a single, scrappy goal late in the game, scored against tired legs and minds.

On this occasion, I was obviously partisan and therefore biased, but even for the casual neutral this game was a classic. Kick-off was, inevitably, at 12pm, prompting one Leeds player to suggest that if we got to the final, it would be played in Los Angeles, behind closed doors at three in the morning. As the TV companies were still beginning to understand the financial benefits of live games, delayed coverage of this one was shown in full at 3pm; time enough for us all to get home after the match and rewatch it, should there be a need. The night before was the most nervous I'd been for any game up to that point, and trying to sleep was futile. From about 3am I paced up and down my bedroom, going through various possibilities and permutations and coming up with nothing solid. I was an emotional mess and would have struggled to predict dawn breaking, never mind the outcome of a closely matched football game. I set off for the stadium having had little sleep but running on nervous energy.

The day itself was almost perfect. The sun shone brightly on Hillsborough, the ground was huge and imposing (if a little dated in a lot of areas), and the mood of the Leeds supporters was optimistic, although not as blindly so as that emanating from our opponents. The local paper – yes, the very same turncoat from the early rounds – produced a special edition on the semi-final with interviews from many senior players. There was a sense of possibility, of enjoying an occasion that only goalkeeper Mervyn

Day had experienced before. Coventry's local press also produced a special edition on the match, and I managed to get a copy from a local newsagent. The difference in mood was startling. As the admittedly superior team Coventry's confidence was expected, even inevitable, but this was something different. The arrogance in their players' interviews was staggering. The semi-final was merely a stepping stone to the ultimate prize; the only way they could be beaten was if they missed the coach. A couple of players paid some respect to their inferior opponents, but it was grudging and without any real belief. Coventry City were going to the FA Cup final; it was as simple as that.

Whether the Leeds players saw the piece or not, I have no idea, but they certainly paid no heed to Coventry's script. As long-odds underdogs with nothing to lose, they tore into Coventry from the start with the same fast, direct football that had given QPR so many problems. John Pearson, still to register his first goal since his January move from Charlton Athletic, forced Coventry keep Steve Ogrizovic into a tremendous early save with a bullet header; defender Brian Burrows then swept the rebound off Ian Baird's toes as he was about to tap into an empty net. Andy Ritchie fired just over and Leeds forced a succession of corners as Coventry struggled to get out of their own half. From one of those corners, David Rennie, only playing for the cup-tied Mark Aizlewood, found space and headed home powerfully at the near post. Two sides of the ground erupted whilst the other two remained incredulously silent. The underdogs were ahead and well on top with only fifteen minutes gone. You would have thought this would wake Coventry from their complacent slumber, but not a chance. Leeds continued to press, Ritchie went close again, Coventry striker Keith Houchen clearly handled the ball in his own penalty area, but neither Leeds players nor their supporters made any great appeals for a penalty. I didn't even see it myself until I saw the highlights later, but even the commentators thought it was obvious. Ogrizovic then produced a save from Ormsby which I have never seen bettered in any game by an opposing goalkeeper. Ormsby struck sweetly, maybe too sweetly from twelve yards, and Ogrizovic, going the wrong way at first, adjusted and, falling back, managed to fling an outstretched arm towards the ball and direct it out for yet another corner. I was directly in front of this at the other end of the stadium and it seemed like a goal all the way. It was very similar in make-up to the famous Banks save from Pelé: a certain goal, a flailing, desperate arm, and a stunning save.

Twenty-five minutes in and Leeds were giving top-flight Coventry a hiding. I think the save was a turning point, though. Disbelieving Leeds players had the wind knocked out of them a little and Coventry realised that, if they wanted to go to Wembley, they were going to have to play some football after all. Towards the end of the half, Coventry got a foothold in the game. Their striker Cyrille Regis missed a couple of good chances and their cup talisman Keith Houchen fired wide from a good position. Houchen had scored the winner at Old Trafford in the fourth round and two at Sheffield Wednesday in the sixth, despite scoring only one league goal all season. He usually put away those chances in the cup – could this be Leeds' day? Leeds still led at half-time, and deservedly so: they had taken the game to their opponents and, with just a touch of luck, would have been out of sight by then. A real sense of possibility was growing in the Leppings Lane End. Not probability – we'd been Leeds fans too long for that – but we'd given ourselves a great chance.

The first part of the second half played out like a standard semi-final, Leeds trying to contain and not chase a game they'd essentially already won; something that had been levelled at them a few times during the season. Coventry looked short on ideas and resorted to pumping long balls upfield for their speedy forwards to chase. I only became aware of this while watching the replay of the game later. I spent most of the second half looking at the clock; every minute seemed like an hour, but the time kept ticking onwards. Leeds got to the midway point of the second half with very little trouble, and then three important figures took centre stage. First, Ron Atkinson, who was now between jobs and occasionally worked as a media pundit. Working alongside commentator Martin Tyler, he was the resident expert for this game. Obviously, while in the stadium I was unaware of this, but around the sixty-five-minute mark, Atkinson remarked that if Coventry didn't change their approach soon the game would be beyond them. The tempter of fate delivered his sermon. Second, enter Brendon Ormsby. He had been in imperious form all season, and especially in the FA Cup. His late goal against QPR had sent Leeds into the quarters and, as mentioned earlier, he'd almost sealed the semi-final with a tremendous shot. With sixty-eight minutes on the clock, Coventry sent yet another hopeful ball forward, running harmlessly into touch with Ormsby shielding it from Coventry's dangerous winger Dave Bennett. As the ball was about to go out, Bennett threw a hopeful leg behind Ormsby and managed to flick the ball back into play. Ormsby fell over Bennett's leg, leaving Bennett free on the byline. Enter character number three. Micky Gynn was a popular figure among Coventry fans but usually confined to the role of impact sub; a role he performed admirably. Up to this point, save for a ten-minute period in the first half, Coventry had failed to trouble Leeds. Gynn, despite not being regarded as a player capable of having an impact over a full ninety minutes, had one thing Leeds feared and were weak against: pace. The Leeds defence was strong, experienced, good in the air but a little slow. They relied on reading and positioning. Against Gynn's fresh legs they had no defence. His impact was immediate: having been on the pitch for only a couple of minutes, he reacted quickly to Bennett retrieving the ball and calmly slotted home his low pass. The explosion of relief from the home end was a scream rather than a roar. Leeds fans fell silent, knowing that their chance had probably gone. Ormsby held his head in his hands.

Many have vilified Ormsby for his supposed aberration, but this is short-sighted. He was doing what every defender who has ever played the game has done: merely seeing the ball out of play. Had he sent it back to Day, conceded a corner and the opposition scored he would again have been to blame. Ninety-nine times out of a hundred he would have got away with it, but this was that one occasion. Bennett, perhaps sensing subconsciously that Atkinson was right, had a late throw of the dice, it came off, and he took the opportunity exceedingly well, remaining calm when the opportunity he'd created opened up for him. There would have been no semi-final for Leeds but for Brendon Ormsby, and laying the blame at his door alone is incredibly stupid and ignorant. Admittedly, his decision changed the course of the game, but much earlier than that he'd changed the course of the entire tournament for Leeds. With just a slight twist of fate this would have been Ormsby's day for all the right reasons.

Coventry had been thrown an unexpected lifeline and were invigorated. Leeds, perhaps sensing the Twin Towers disappearing out of sight, looked dejected and, to be honest, beaten. The game turned full circle and Coventry began to run Leeds into the ground. Gynn spread terror with his runs through the middle; Bennett began to torment former teammate Micky Adams like a sadistic cat playing with an injured mouse. He started to go by Adams at will, and Leeds hung on desperately. Houchen had a goal-bound shot blocked on the six-yard line, and there were many others as Coventry swarmed forward, smelling blood. Seventy-eight minutes on the clock and the inevitable happened. Another long run from Gynn, Houchen took the ball into the area, and Ormsby, looking to make up for his earlier error, swung a wild foot and missed completely. Houchen rounded Day and slotted into the far corner. Everything had turned and now Coventry were indeed heading to Wembley. The Leeds fans were silent and dejected, expecting the worst, and turned their minds to damage limitation for the last ten minutes. The next few minutes followed in the same vein. Coventry were rampant and Regis should really have sealed it when he went around Day and tried an unnecessary step over before firing into the side netting. Another sign of Coventry's complacency creeping back in, perhaps, but it looked like it would make no difference. Despite Regis's embarrassing miss it all looked to be over. It had been a spirited effort but Coventry had full control now and there was only one possible outcome.

There is one more cameo to introduce here. Leeds striker Keith Edwards had been a prolific striker in the second tier for both Sheffield United and Hull City. He'd signed for Leeds in the summer of 1986 and it was felt that he would be able to provide the consistent stream of goals that had seemed beyond the likes of Baird and Ritchie. In Leeds colours this proved not to be the case: for large parts of his Leeds career Edwards looked slow and unfit. It took him six games to score his first goal, he missed a penalty in the League Cup at Oldham Athletic, and by the semi-final he had only four Leeds goals to his name and was a rare starter. Him coming on with less than ten minutes to go in a game in which Leeds were behind and completely overrun did nothing to assuage the Leeds supporters' apathy, and his arrival was greeted with a polite if somewhat resigned applause. The game was over, we'd put up a good fight, and now it was time to just blow the whistle and let us go home.

As with Gynn, though, Edwards' impact was immediate. With seven minutes to go, Leeds' best player on the day, Andy Ritchie, managed to wriggle past three challenges on the right-hand byline in front of the Leeds supporters with a combination of dogged determination and a slice of luck. I would like to say that he used exquisite skill, but that would really be stretching a point. With the same calmness Bennett had showed fifteen minutes before, Ritchie crossed for the head of Edwards, who headed powerfully and low past Ogrizovic. I wish I could pretend that I was right behind the goal when Edwards placed his header; I'm sure he has been told that by at least fifty thousand people since. But as I said earlier, I was off to the right of the stand and in line with Ritchie, though I couldn't see him for the mass of people in front of me. The cross seemed to come out of nowhere and I could only see Edwards' head as he nodded it home, and nothing of the ball as it nestled in the bottom corner. I only knew what had happened by the reaction to my right.

I could go on forever, explaining my reaction and that of other Leeds fans to this goal, but it would be much easier to look it up on YouTube and watch it for yourself. I do this frequently – maybe twice a week – and it never fails to send a shiver down my spine. The reaction of the fans in the Leppings Lane End is one that will never leave me. If you attend, say, five hundred games in your life and you follow a relatively unsuccessful team you will probably have moments like this on maybe half a dozen occasions. Times when your emotions take you over, when you hug complete strangers, when you are totally incapable of holding back tears of joy, when you have absolutely no control over or any idea of what you are doing. All that emotion just for an equaliser, but such is the passion of the FA Cup. Many Coventry City fans have commented since that ITV commentator Martin Tyler was biased towards Leeds that day. They cite his reaction to the Leeds goal, screaming, "*Edwards!*", followed by, "A game that was always memorable has now become wonderful." Do you know what, Coventry fans? You are one hundred per cent correct. Tyler started his career with Yorkshire Television, often covering Leeds, before moving to mainstream ITV, then Sky Sports. As the best and only top-flight team in Yorkshire when I started following them, Leeds were often on ITV's regional equivalent of *Match of the Day* and, along with John Helm, Tyler was part of the main commentary team. I spent many Sundays listening to his erudite, informed commentary. So yes, he was unashamedly biased; even I could see that. But you had the rest of the country on your side, so I think our conscience is clear.

With parity restored, both teams went at it again for the last eight minutes, but by now everyone was way too tired to make a positive impact. David Rennie had a decent shot saved comfortably by Ogrizovic, but there was nothing else of note. Extra time passed in the same cagey semi-final style as the second half, but not without drama. With a scrappy effort, Bennett gave Coventry the lead in the first half of extra time. The rest of the game played out amid a growing sense of inevitability. Coventry looked comfortable despite their fatigue and Leeds looked spent. Coventry fans sang their version of the 'Eton Boating Song' and celebrated wildly. They were going to Wembley; they knew it and we knew it. We'd given a great account of ourselves and the fans had also behaved, showing incredible vocal support.

The drama wasn't quite over, though. With the last kick of the game, Edwards found space in the box and Ogrizovic yet again produced an incredible save; almost a last-ditch equaliser from a team who'd given everything. The game ended and the Leeds players collapsed, exhausted, to the ground. The supporters, maybe too exhausted themselves to riot, tried their best to raise their spirits and even matched the celebrating Coventry fans for noise. I was devastated and proud at the same time. I couldn't stem my tears of frustration but that semi-final was and still is one of my top five moments watching Leeds. Paradoxically, for a number of reasons I'm glad Edwards didn't equalise. If it had been a winner then of course I would have taken it, but actually I didn't want an equaliser because I felt that Coventry would have had our number for the replay. There would have been no complacent start and Coventry were a very good team that season. Beating Tottenham in the final, Manchester United in an earlier round, and Tottenham, Everton and Liverpool in the league bears that out. Our lads had given everything and in a replay Coventry would have given them a bit of a pasting. Far better to keep the memories of a close, engrossing game and the dreams of what might have been.

Another reason was that this was so stereotypically Leeds. The club has a largely deserved reputation for choking. Even though the great, famous side won six trophies they were runners-up eleven times, no matter what the ageing romantics might tell you. To be so close, then mess it all up, was what we were all about. I didn't start supporting Leeds to see them win every week; I wanted somewhere to go where my self-pity would be complete and others would understand. Losing in this way is what defines us. Had we got the replay and taken the inevitable beating, I don't think I would remember the first game with the same fondness. And remembering a defeat with fondness is part of our make-up, however much we crave success and claim otherwise.

This was also the day when, in the eyes of many, things started to change for Leeds. In front of the nation they had put up a stunning and probably slightly unlucky performance. The supporters had been very well behaved and could be heard throughout the game. Even for the most obviously biased it was difficult not to feel for them. Then at the end, something happened to bring all this together, and the Coventry players can take great credit for this. Four of them approached the Leeds supporters and started to applaud them. Not in a 'We won; fuck you' kind of way, but to say, 'You guys put up a hell of a fight today.' The Leeds fans were appreciative and, knowing that both sides had played their part in a fantastic encounter, rose as one to applaud the Coventry players. No booing, just two different sides acknowledging the other's part in a great day when no one deserved to lose but someone had to. Well, they didn't – there was always the possibility of a replay – but I explained that earlier.

The media played up these events and, although they generally hated Leeds, even they recognised the parts both team and supporters had played on the day. For days afterwards I read the papers avidly and basked in the glow of positive reinforcement from a usually hostile media. We Leeds fans tend to revel in the bad-boy, badly-done-to image, but being hated all the time is exhausting and sometimes it's nice to have nice things said about you, no matter how much you may deny it.

LEEDS UNITED V BRADFORD CITY, SATURDAY 28TH FEBRUARY 1987

BACK TO THE LEAGUE: THE PLAY-OFF CAMPAIGN, AND ILL-JUDGED CHOICES

This game was played before the quarter-final against Wigan Athletic and would normally have been omitted from this book, but for perhaps the most bizarre incident I ever witnessed at a football match.

The game itself, although a Yorkshire derby, was uneventful. The only two things of note were Keith Edwards' last-minute winner for Leeds and Don Goodman failing to score against us for once, although he did hit the bar. Goodman was known as a real nemesis of Leeds and a regular scorer against them for Bradford, West Bromwich Albion, Sunderland and Wolves. He'd only played once for Wolves against Leeds, in a 1998 FA Cup quarter-final at Elland Road. Leeds were in the top five in the premiership and Wolves mid-table in the Second Division. Before the game I'd been confident – not Coventry confident, but still confident. Then I found out that Goodman was playing for Wolves and my confidence drained. I just knew. Was I right? I don't want to talk about it; that game was almost as painful as the semi-final defeat, and you can find it on the internet too.

Anyway, I digress. As I say, this was just a standard Yorkshire derby, but the main event occurred before the game. Outside the stadium, Mars were giving away free samples of their new Tracker cereal bar. A good marketing ploy, giving out essentially healthy options at football stadiums, where snack options were either crisps or Wagon Wheels. When they are free and being distributed by pretty young girls to impressionable wannabe teenage hooligans and young football obsessives, I would say so. The Leeds fans outside the Kop took their gifts gratefully, albeit with a little bemusement. They were used to having things taken off them before they entered the stadium, not given to them. Most of us stuffed our bar in a pocket and forgot all about it.

Before the game there was a presentation on the pitch for February's Player of the Month. This was usually done by a former player or legend, or maybe a local famous person or dignitary. This time, though, the Leeds board outdid themselves and went for a big name, but their choice was just plain bizarre. I forget who the player in receipt of the award was – probably Sheridan again, or maybe Ormsby for his cup heroics – but the announcer managed to get the attention of the Leeds crowd. "So here to present the award, we have the man who predicted our fifth-round win against QPR. Please welcome Emlyn Hughes!" This was true – Hughes had predicted the victory – but he'd also said at the third-round stage that Leeds should be kicked out of the tournament simply for having too many supporters. There was a moment of stunned silence, then howls of derision filled the stadium as the Leeds support showed their disgust. I showed mine as I always do in situations like this: by looking up to the heavens and shaking my head. Despite my ambivalence towards my nation, I can be archetypically British sometimes. The rest of the Leeds fans in the Kop that day had their own unique way of demonstrating their displeasure. The first thing I saw when I looked up was not the stadium roof, but hundreds of Tracker bars sailing through the air like a New York ticker-tape parade. There was no hope of them reaching Hughes or the Leeds officials, unless Olympic shot-putter Geoff Capes was throwing them. It was just a natural reaction to a ridiculous, short-sighted decision. No coins, knives, darts or fireworks: Tracker bars. Many landed at the bottom of the stand, to be greeted with some amusement by the fans down there, who were used to dodging fireworks and other equally lethal projectiles. Cellophane wrapper cuts can be damaging, though.

"How did you get your face cut; Bradford's Ointment boys take a knife to you?"

"No, actually; I came under attack from a tasty, healthy chocolate alternative." Not a story to tell down the local.

What were Hughes and the Leeds board thinking? Did the board not read the papers? As for Hughes, while it's impolite to speak ill of the dead, it takes a special kind of arrogance to tell someone they are cheats and a disgrace to football and then walk onto their pitch and expect to be accepted with open arms. Just ask Brian Clough. But what can you expect from a man who was hated by his own teammates? Liverpool defender and hard man Tommy Smith's relationship with Hughes made Andy Cole and Teddy Sheringham look like Ant and Dec. There is a famous (and possibly apocryphal) story about Smith and Leeds striker Allan Clarke, who had – shall we say? – an acrimonious relationship. Clarke had upended Hughes during a Leeds–Liverpool game and saw Smith striding purposefully towards him. Fearing the worst, Clarke braced himself for a confrontation. When Smith reached Clarke, he apparently told him to give Hughes kick from him the next time he got close enough.

I usually take stories like this, however entertaining, with a pinch of salt, but I've never wanted a story to be true as much as I wanted that one to be. Whilst no one should have to suffer the dreadful illness that took Hughes' life, it doesn't change the fact that throughout his career he was generally considered, even by his teammates, to be a complete dick. I would, however, like to thank him for his contribution to the most memorable non-football moment I've had at Elland Road. However ill judged his appearance may have been, it gave a tepid match an engaging memory, surpassing even the late winner.

LEEDS UNITED V IPSWICH TOWN, SATURDAY 18TH APRIL 1987

BEATING THATCHER TO THE ID CARD

The first home game after the semi-final, and the appetite of the locals had certainly been whetted as twenty-five thousand filed into Elland Road. Leeds had dragged themselves into contention for a play-off place and Ipswich Town were their main rivals. The game played out in bright sunshine and the cup tragedy was quickly forgotten as Leeds raced into a two-goal lead. Ipswich pulled one back, then Brendon Ormsby redeemed himself after his cup transgression by adding a third before Ipswich scored another late on. They almost snatched a point as well: Leeds defender Bobby McDonald, who earlier had scored his first and only goal for the club, managed a sublime goal-line clearance by taking a point-blank shot full in the face. Leeds took the points and maintained their play-off push, albeit perhaps through fortune rather than skill. After the previous week, though, even the most biased supporter couldn't begrudge them a stroke of luck. The cup run was over and promotion was starting to enter the minds of the faithful for the first time since relegation five years before.

The other thing that occurred at this time was Leeds United becoming the first club to incorporate a membership scheme. The

U Club card (U, I expect, standing for United) was a poorly made paper card, laminated in plastic, with a photo and a name on the front. This allowed the holder to purchase one ticket per away game. The qualifications for obtaining the card were somewhat exacting. As with previous away ticket restrictions they were only available to season ticket holders and supporters' club members, but with the addendum that holders would only be given a card when the club had received two character references. Chants about going to Wembley were soon replaced with "If you haven't got a reference clap your hands."

This rule was strictly enforced: one of my references failed to come through and, as a result, my card failed to materialise until a friend went to the ground and filled one out for me. This meant I didn't get my card until the season had almost finished, and so attending an away game with one of the most notorious bands of supporters in the land carried a similar vetting process to that of an exclusive Mayfair gentlemen's club. Still, anything that could help the club keep out the hooligans who had come close to killing it was going to be well received by the well-behaved majority.

The system worked very well as trouble almost evaporated, but for the enterprising there were still ways around it. As I say, the cards were very poorly made. At the beginning of the 1988–9 season, I'd stupidly lost mine and had to get another. A backlog meant the cards were late arriving and I didn't have mine in time for the first away game at Portsmouth. Not to be outdone, I got someone who had a card but wasn't attending the match to buy a ticket, sell it to me, and loan me his card. I then cling-filmed my photo over his and put the card in an old transparent Yorkshire Bank card holder, went down to Portsmouth and took my chances. During the five-hour journey, given time for reflection, I decided this was a terrible, ill-thought-out idea. I was obviously going to be caught and probably banned from future away games, just for the sake of one game almost three hundred miles away. What was I thinking? After a few beers in a pub near the ground I was brave enough to give my plan a try. I was hoping to be stopped by a steward, who would be expected to give the card a cursory glance and then let me in. I was, however, stopped by a police inspector, who paid my wallet far more attention than I was comfortable with. Luckily, he didn't take the card out of the case and I got in unscathed and took my place on the terraces, taking time to still my pounding heart.

Was it worth making a six-hundred-mile round trip, committing fraud and risking arrest and prosecution, just to see my beloved team in action? A 4–0 hiding would suggest otherwise, but sometimes you have to take the risk, remember the experience and forget the result.

LEEDS UNITED V WEST BROMWICH ALBION, MONDAY 4TH MAY 1987

PLAY-OFF CONFIRMATION, AND AN EGO TRIP FOR SHERIDAN
A run of seven straight home wins meant that a play-off place was secured easier than would have been expected in February when we floundered around in mid-table, with Leeds finishing six points clear of sixth-place Crystal Palace. Had Leeds produced any sort of decent away form they might not have needed the play-offs. However, they tempered being top home scorers with second-lowest away scorers and finished with a paltry fifteen goals and only four wins. As a result, they finished ten points behind second-place Portsmouth.

The play-offs were confirmed in this last home game of the season against West Bromwich Albion, with a 3–2 win in a game in which Leeds were more comfortable than the scoreline suggested. The game was played out in bright spring sunshine and John Pearson managed to score his first goal at Elland Road. He was later to become a target for the boo boys due to his goal output, but this was a period of untold positivity for Leeds United and even his paltry goal total for a striker was forgiven as new and exciting times emerged.

The only other noteworthy event during this match was the Leeds supporters invading the pitch, as used to happen occasionally at the last game. I cannot remember there ever being anything to celebrate at a last match but maybe for mid-table nonentities that is the point. We invest so much time in something which is to a large extent meaningless, so maybe we deserve our moment just as much as the trophy hunters do. Who says we don't have the right to celebrate being stuck in no man's land since November? Or maybe we are celebrating not having to think about football for another three months and being able to live like normal human beings? This sense of freedom usually lasts until the middle of June, when we start to miss football terribly and ache for the fixtures to come out, but we deserve our moment as much as the winners are allowed their celebrations and the losers are allowed to grieve.

I only remember invading the pitch once, for a home game against Charlton Athletic at the end of the 1983-4 season when Eddie Gray retired. I decided that was a great reason to scale the ten-foot, spike-topped fence and jump onto the pitch. An elderly steward made no effort to stop me, probably hoping I'd impale myself. When I landed safely beside him, he lamented that Eddie's retirement wasn't complemented by a return to the big time.

"Ah! Next year, definitely," I breezed cheerfully.

He shook his head dolefully at my youthful, naive and misguided optimism and returned to watching other supporters trying to impale themselves, while I ran off giddily to the West Stand to say goodbye to a player who wasn't going anywhere because he was still the club's manager.

This season, though, three years later, the supporters had every right to invade the sacred territory. As far as success went there had been nothing even close to it for over a decade, and though there was still work to be done, this was more than we'd dared dream about in January. I didn't enter the pitch this time – I was too high up on the terraces to consider making my way down, and felt better basking in the relative glory from where I was; a smug look on my face as I watched a few hundred take their chances with the stewards and the infamous spikes. It was just standard end-of-season stuff and would normally have passed without the need for additional comment. The supporters usually mooched around for a while, not really knowing what to do without anything definite to celebrate, and then trundled quietly off home as the stadium emptied.

This, however, was no normal season. A group of about fifty surrounded the season's hero John Sheridan, hoisted him high on someone's shoulders and proceeded to escort him on a lap of honour. Sheridan wore an expression that was equally amused and petrified in case he was dropped, and the most telling memory for me is him putting his hands out constantly to steady himself. Rapturous applause followed this piece of ingenuity around the stadium, and I'm sure Sheridan remembers it to this day and it will have taken his ego a long time to play it down. I expect his bemused teammates watching from the sides were only too happy to help, though.

THE PLAY-OFFS

This was the first season of the play-offs. The idea was for it to be a temporary tournament designed to lower the number of top-flight clubs from twenty-two to twenty over the next two years. So, it was decided that, in order to lose an extra club in the first season, the bottom three in the First Division would be relegated and the top two promoted automatically. Then the clubs in third, fourth and fifth place would go into the play-offs with the nineteenth club in the top flight. Therefore, it would be either three up and four down, or two up and three down. Charlton Athletic from the First Division would play fifth-place Ipswich Town, while third-place Oldham Athletic would play fourth-place Leeds. The winners would then play in a two-legged tie for the last place in the First

Division. Until 1990, in these early seasons of the play-offs there was no extra incentive of a Wembley final. Oldham could have some justification in feeling hard done by. They had finished third, seven points above Leeds, and in the previous season would have been promoted comfortably. But changes are changes and they wouldn't have had any complaints had they finished fifth and been promoted. It could also be said that playing their home games on a plastic pitch gave them an unfair advantage.

There was an argument amongst the purists about their brand of football, too. Their manager Joe Royle eventually got them playing some fantastic, swaggering football a few years later, but this was not the case in the early days. Oldham were successful but dour to watch, playing constant back passes to their admittedly brilliant keeper Andy Goram, and used a tediously boring offside trap, interestingly named "condensing the field of play" by Royle.

Leeds and Oldham also had some history. These home and away encounters would be the sixth time the clubs had met during the season, and they actually played each other ten times between April 1986 and November 1987. Add to this Oldham's sense of injustice, and their having former Leeds players Andy Linighan, Denis Irwin and Tommy Wright in their side, and this was certainly a case of familiarity breeding contempt.

Although bristling with raw emotion, the play-off matches were as as turgid and tight as FA Cup semi-finals. The teams were so closely matched in all cases that they rarely produced open, flowing football. Due to what was at stake, though, they proved to be intoxicating, high-octane events, and what had started as a temporary system to reduce the number of clubs in the First Division became an important permanent fixture in the football calendar. The second-tier play-off final eventually replaced the FA Cup final as the last game of the season.

The two games against Oldham were tense, often violent, and in the end fraught with late drama. Once again, enter the early-season failure Keith Edwards. He seemed to find his feet a little after Hillsborough, and started to hit the net. Not with the same frivolity as in his earlier days at other clubs, but they were still important goals. In both games here, he left it late.

LEEDS UNITED V OLDHAM ATHLETIC, PLAY-OFF SEMI-FINAL FIRST LEG, THURSDAY 14TH MAY 1987

FULL STADIUMS AND LATE DRAMA

The biggest crowd for a league fixture since 1983 flocked to Elland Road as everyone looked to put the disappointment of the cup defeat behind them. No one expected anything but a tight game given Oldham's reputation and, due to the respective performances in the league, I suspect everyone secretly felt that Oldham had the edge. A long run of successive home victories for Leeds gave cause for optimism, though, and it was felt that taking even a slight lead into the away game would give us at least a fighting chance. This was a new experience for all the supporters and the noise in the ground was deafening, even surpassing that at the QPR game. Even if the odds were against us, we were going to give it a real go, and everyone hoped the players would be suitably inspired.

As expected, Leeds were frustrated by Oldham's spoiling tactics and the game threatened to boil over into mayhem as the teams started to regard the ball as incidental, with high boots, late tackles and flailing elbows the order of the day. The only attacking points of note were a deflected Sheridan shot against the bar and couple of decent saves by Goram. Entering the last minute, Leeds got a free kick just outside the area but to the right, out of Sheridan's normal shooting range. He stood over it and drilled a low, fast ball into the centre of the box. Edwards dived full length at it and deflected a header past Goram, and the whole home section exploded in relief. So, another home win to make it eight in a row and an outside chance of making the final, which before Edwards' late intervention had looked unlikely. Maybe, just maybe, it would be our year after all, despite the heartache of the semi-final defeat. The trip to Boundary Park, however, was expected to be daunting.

OLDHAM ATHLETIC V LEEDS UNITED, PLAY-OFF SEMI-FINAL SECOND LEG, SUNDAY 17TH MAY 1987

AGAINST ALL ODDS

Football fans are hugely superstitious and have a strong belief in portents. These superstitions tend to be personal. I will only drink in certain pubs before a game, I will not bet on or against my team, and a few years ago I took to wearing odd socks at every game after wearing a pair for the trip to Anfield for Alan Smith's famous debut goal against Liverpool in 1998. My main ritual, though, takes place inside the stadium. I usually stand behind one of the goals. When the teams come out, the fans on the sides can see them approaching and start to applaud, and the rest of the crowd follows suit in expectation. I cannot do this; I must see at least three white shirts before I raise my hands. I have to confess that the reason for this escapes me and the practice rarely works, but I do it anyway.

Equally, personal moods and luck are thought by many to influence a game, although clearly this must be nonsense: Leeds' 7–2 drubbing at Stoke would imply that something like fifty thousand people from the same city had had the week from hell leading up to the game. I certainly did, but surely this can't have been the case for everyone. Someone who attended that game must have gone there in a decent mood, even though it would have evaporated long before half-time. I remember attending a cup game at Aston Villa many years later, after a particularly bitter and nasty argument with my soon-to-be ex girlfriend. I arrived at the stadium in a terrible state and even a dominant first-half display and a 2–1 lead could not raise me from my depression. Everyone else in the Leeds end was jubilant but I couldn't share their joy. Leeds went on to lose the game and prove my point, but this also gave me the feeling that the result was entirely my fault. This makes the supporters' relationship with their club entirely personal. They feel that their moods are reflected in the club's fortunes.

It is strange, though, that this effect is confined to negative moods. I can remember a few occasions when my mood was so low that I felt it was impossible for the club to get a positive result. I cannot, however, remember one single occasion when I felt euphoric about something and the club followed suit and produced one of their one-in-a-hundred moments. There is a case to be made that most of my ecstatic moments have been tied to the club and therefore there were very few in my personal life that might influence Leeds United's performance. In the past this would have been a valid point, but living abroad has helped me to put some emotional as well as physical distance between myself and the club. I am no longer a dangerous obsessive; merely a sometimes overly passionate fan. There is still that nagging feeling, though, that our fortunes are intrinsically linked. For me the club plays a sinister, almost Devil's advocate role in this process. When I'm at my lowest they seem to insist on dragging me down a little further, refusing point-blank to gain a decent result no matter how well the odds are stacked in their favour.

It doesn't work the other way, though. Whilst living in China I started dating a stunning Chinese girl, quite a bit younger than me (she was thirty years old to my fifty-two), whom I had known for a long time and never thought I would get close to. Yet there we were, and she seemed as keen on me as I was on her. I was in a football-free euphoric stupor and couldn't quite believe my luck. My romantic life had never been so good, and I lived in a semi-conscious daydream. Barely anything could lower my mood. I say 'barely' because we started dating the day before the second-leg play-off semi-final against Derby County in 2019. With a 1–0 first-leg lead and another early goal in the second leg, Leeds looked set to reach the play-off final with consummate ease and, for once, reflect my positive mood. They were having none of it, though, and, in traditional Leeds style, proceeded to throw it away and choke. In my youth this would have crushed me, despite my romantic success, but maybe middle-aged maturity or perhaps a five-thousand-mile distance made the pain much less acute. Disappointment, a shrug of the shoulders, and that was it. In fact, I almost found it funny because it was so typically Leeds. It's easy to feel this way when you have other things going on in your life, and in my youth, when Leeds United were the fulcrum of my existence, it would have destroyed me for weeks. Once, I would have fully expected to lose the girl too, but by then I knew that wouldn't happen. Part of this self-fulfilling prophecy was probably due to the fact that in my youth I might have taken the poor result out on the girl, seen her as a bad omen and expected the worst. By that point, however, while I still cared about football, I cared about my girlfriend more, and there was always the next season. It was also helpful that she came from a continent where football isn't played or watched with any real enthusiasm. She had no interest in the sport and no idea who my team are. It never came up in conversation. In England, girls I dated would be vaguely aware of my team and usually either show a total lack of understanding or, in the case of the more shameful ones, take the piss. My Chinese girlfriend having no knowledge of something that matters so much to me was actually helpful and meant that I could keep the two apart. We actually split up halfway through the promotion season that followed, and it hurt us both intensely. Neither of us wanted it; cultural problems and familial loyalties on her part got in the way and the choice was taken away from us. It hurt much more than the Derby defeat, and even though promotion has been achieved at last I still miss her terribly and spend as much time looking at photos of us together as I do watching Pablo Hernández's winner at Swansea or Stuart Dallas's winner at Man City in the first season back. Wild ecstasy and heart-wrenching agony from the same period of time. It would seem that my personal life and my team's fortunes are not linked after all.

When I was still a callow youth, though, this level of perception and forward thinking was beyond me and Leeds United mattered to me like nothing else. This is the problem for every ultra-keen football fan, and at the time of the Oldham game I had absolutely nothing else going on my life. Football was my sole motivation. Taking all this into account, the Oldham game had all the elements of a disaster. Oldham had beaten Leeds three times that season. Leeds had gained a 1–0 win at Boundary Park in a league game in December, but even the most biased Leeds fan would confess that it was somewhat fortunate. Add in the advantage of Oldham's plastic pitch, for which Leeds players showed undisguised loathing, and the slender single-goal advantage didn't look like enough. On a personal front, I had no girlfriend and no job, but I'd had neither for the entirety of the season, so that had no real effect. There were other outside forces, though. I had started travelling to games by car with a new group of fellow fans. We were due to drive down to Boundary Park in relative comfort. The car broke down in midweek, though, and as all the park-and-ride places had been taken it was a mad dash to find alternative transport. In those pre-internet days, this was easier said than done. There were no available trains or coaches going to Oldham. National Express were running a service to nearby Chadderton, but only one bus that would get there at 8.30am, three and a half hours before kick-off. The ground was roughly a thirty-minute walk away, so this meant a long wait at the stadium. At least we could look forward to a quiet, comfortable coach ride. Who wants to travel from Leeds to Chadderton at 7am on a Sunday morning? Yes, another Sunday-noon kick-off. Well, apparently another fifty or so Leeds fans had the same idea, so rather than a charming low-key journey through the picturesque Pennines, the trip was a raucous celebration full of endless chanting. The fans on the bus were in exuberant mood and none seemed to share my fear.

The rest of the time up to kick-off was uneventful except for one thing. The Manchester region upheld its reputation for dreariness and it never stopped raining from our leaving the coach to kick-off; indeed, for the whole of the game. But it was only a light drizzle and, with Oldham having an all-weather plastic pitch, the game went ahead, although it was delayed half an hour to let in all the latecomers. In 1987 the Boundary Park away stand was an open terrace so there was no escape from the rain, but as kick-off approached that was quickly forgotten. What was apparent was the number of Leeds fans in the crowd. There were almost as many Leeds supporters as Oldham ones, and plenty more who had obtained tickets for the Oldham end. Although this game was bound to end in defeat there would be others with whom to share it, and so the pain would be diluted somewhat.

For their part, Leeds played to the script and Oldham controlled the game, taking more readily to the familiar surface. The inevitable happened at eighteen minutes when a loose ball fell to the edge of the box and an Oldham midfielder stroked it home with embarrassing ease. The scores were level and we were all ready for capitulation and a drubbing. But due to Leeds' unusual determination and a combination of bad luck and bad finishing on the part of Oldham, these failed to materialise. Yes, Oldham dominated possession, but the nearest to a goal was an Ian Baird shot against the post, which almost gave the game to Leeds. The game entered the last minute and although confidence wasn't high, at least extra time beckoned and we had taken the game all the way. It is at these times that football can be at its most cruel. If Oldham had scored on seventy-five minutes, we would have been hurt and dismayed, but it was coming and we were pretty much outplayed anyway. Most supporters would agree that the raw emotion of a last-minute winner beats a 5–0 win any day of the week. Add in the high stakes of an all-or-nothing play-off semi-final and those feelings are multiplied. What happened at Boundary Park in the next minute will live forever with everyone who was there to witness it, and serves as a pure example of football's combination of extreme pleasure and pain. Less than thirty seconds to go and Mike Cecere, the Oldham substitute, rose unmarked in the box and powered home a comfortable header, leaving Mervyn Day stranded. The Oldham end exploded; Joe Royle and former Leeds player Tommy Wright were dancing on the pitch. It was game over. I had been standing in the rain since 8.30 and it was now 2.15. I was drenched and watching the Oldham faithful jumping around with all the demented glee a last-minute winner in an all-or-nothing game is likely to generate. In a few seconds the season flashed before my eyes. I'd been to every home game and a dozen away games. We were twenty-two minutes from the FA Cup final and one game from the play-off final, and a whole season had just evaporated right in front of me.

These are the moments when you truly hate your chosen team or sport. Why did I do this? Why did I put myself through all this pain for this lot; these overpaid, glory-dangling, dream-destroying, choking bastards? My eyes locked on the face of a balding, middle-aged Oldham fan in the stand to my left. His smug countenance was soaking in glory and I hated him for it. He had every right to his bliss – in terms of success, Oldham made us look positively board-sweeping – but I still hated him and everything his crappy, boring, defensive but ultimately successful team had put me through. All my false hope over the preceding nine months had been blown away by a simple last-minute header. At that moment, I never wanted to see another football match ever again.

In vague realisation that the game had restarted I took a baleful glance at the pitch, looking for the referee more than anything, hoping that he would blow his whistle and put an end to this misery so we Leeds supporters could all grieve as one while we waited for the police to let us out and then I could go home and get out of the fucking rain. I didn't see the referee; what I did see was Leeds substitute Keith Edwards struggle free in the area and angle a shot past our goalkeeping nemesis Andy Goram. The ball nestled in the far corner, almost directly in my line of vision. It was at the other end of the pitch and witnessed through driving rain, but is still entrenched in my memory as clear as a photograph.

There is little notice taken of the psychology of these moments, and it's worth considering it from both sides. A last-minute winner or loser is always an emotional thing. Everything is on, then everything is lost, or the other way around: an all-consuming low to an almost immediate fantastic high. I've watched the match online since and timed the goal scored by Edwards: nine seconds from kick-off to the ball hitting the net. The human psyche isn't programmed to accept such instant, polarising change. In all my live games I have never witnessed a crowd go as wild; there was a little bit more room here to hug complete strangers than at Hillsborough and everyone took the opportunity gleefully. I witnessed hard lads with tears running down their cheeks, the rain for once playing its part in hiding their embarrassment, not that there was any. As for the Oldham supporters, even through my elation I felt their heartbreak. Leeds fans had had a little experience of this four years earlier: in an FA Cup tie at home to Arsenal they had taken the lead with two minutes of extra time to go. Arsenal had then equalised a minute later and won the reply. So I could empathise to a point, but this was different. Arsenal had scored at least a minute after Leeds, not nine seconds, and all that had been at stake was a place in the fifth round of a tournament they were extremely unlikely to win. This was a play-off semi-final, one tie away from the promised land of First Division football, something Oldham had never experienced; a season's work coming together and taken away again in a few seconds. The Arsenal game had been heartbreaking in its own way, but not season-defining. After my euphoria died down a little – after all, there was still extra time to come – I looked over at the Oldham fans again and locked onto the same supporter whom I had observed celebrating just a minute earlier. His smile had gone, his expression consumed by gloom. No one should be subjected to such humiliation but it's the price we pay for caring too much. In a neutral situation I would have felt his pain deeply, but this was slowly becoming my day and I had other priorities.

Extra time it was, but under play-off rules, whilst away goals didn't matter in normal time, they became relevant if the scores were tied at the end of extra time. Leeds had the priceless away goal. Extra time passed seamlessly, Oldham seemed way too dejected to put up much of a fight, and despite maybe accusations of a lack of professionalism who can blame them? Former Leeds centre back Andy Linighan hit the top of the bar with a header that Day had well covered but it was a token resistance, and the inevitable whistle came and Leeds supporters and players celebrated like they had won the final itself. After six hundred games I still rank this as my greatest live moment. I've seen Champions League victories against Europe's greatest, wins against Manchester United, and the final home game in 1990 against Leicester City when Gordon Strachan flung an exhausted leg at a sloppy clearance and put Leeds back on course for a promotion that had looked to be slipping away. Nothing, though, has matched the contrasting emotions of that single explosive, season-defining minute.

I thought about the game a lot afterwards and still felt a little sympathy for Oldham. I would have been devastated to finish third in the league in the first season when third wouldn't be good enough, and then go out in the play-offs in such a way. I thought of the balding Oldham supporter and felt for him. But I also thought about Oldham's negative tactics away from home: their dreary back passes, their "condensing the field of play". I remembered Linighan in the League Cup tie at Elland Road, goading Edwards to try and take the ball from him before nonchalantly passing it back to his goalkeeper for the umpteenth time that evening. Then I remembered the advantage of the plastic pitch: Oldham being able to play and train on it all season, to get used to it; a benefit not afforded to the opposition. I thought about Edwards, the very man whom Linighan had goaded at Elland Road, grabbing that last-second lifeline. That priceless away goal that Oldham had shown no interest in pursuing at Elland Road, gained on the plastic pitch that had proved so advantageous to them all season. Then I smiled and thought, *Karma is a bitch, but sometimes she can be such a wonderful, revenge-granting bitch.*

LEEDS UNITED V CHARLTON ATHLETIC, PLAY-OFF FINAL FIRST LEG, SATURDAY 23RD MAY 1987

A NEW BEGINNING AND BOGEY GROUNDS

Something very unusual happened in the run-up to this game; something that startled everyone who knew me – hell, it even took me a little by surprise. I got a job. For the first time in three years, I was regularly and gainfully employed. In those economically uncertain days, Leeds City Council ran a scheme called the Community Programme. This was basically a similar project to the Youth Training Scheme but for adults and with the added attraction of a decent living wage. I decided to shake off my youthful lethargy and applied for a part-time office job, then was surprised to get an interview and even more stunned to be offered the position. I can lay the blame for my inertia at the feet of the Tory government and the Mad Granny of Grantham as much as I like, but that only tells part of the story. The truth is that at the time I was much too lazy to work and way too emotionally unstable to deal with the nuances of workplace politics. I was also stubborn. The more people told me to get a job, the more I dug in my heels and refused. But by this time everyone had given up on me and stopped complaining and haranguing me, so it was obviously time to get myself sorted.

I was probably swept along on the crest of the wave created by my team as well. They too had been inert, lazy, bad-tempered, unpredictable and prone to prolonged bouts of self-pity. It also has to be said that we were both uninspiring, directionless and lacking in ambition. These were different days, though, and I had to fall in line with the new swashbuckling style of my team and get off my arse and do something. To be honest, this was less a natural reaction to the change in approach and style of my beloved club and more to do with the cost of all the extra must-see games. It was only a part-time job and a one-year contract, but I was soon given a full-time position and moved to a different location as a stock controller. I really enjoyed that role, and the experience proved invaluable for the full-time position I secured after leaving the programme. I started in electrical wholesaling at twenty-two years old; my first proper job that wasn't either a training course or a scheme. My family were stunned, pleased, and yet a little exasperated by my sudden embracing of the working world. Why hadn't this happened three years ago, they wanted to know? Because they'd stopped bothering me about it, was my churlish answer.

So, Leeds United were flying high in the play-off final, playing the best football anyone had seen at Elland Road since Tony Currie left, the fans were behaving, both were receiving muted and slightly begrudging praise from the media and neutrals, and Neville had a job. All we needed was for Margaret Thatcher to sit down for a coffee with Ronald Reagan and discuss the merits of socialism and the turnaround would have been complete. I even approached the Charlton tie with a degree of confidence. There were a few parallels from the previous round against Oldham. Charlton had finished nineteenth in the First Division in their first season back, and normally this would have kept them safe, so they approached the tie with the same kind of disgruntlement as the

Oldham fans had. There had also been a couple of recent player movements between the two clubs, but this time the other way. Striker John Pearson and midfielder Mark Aizlewood had joined Leeds from Charlton in January, and both had made a steady if unspectacular start. As Leeds had come so close to beating a Coventry side that had finished in the top ten and beaten a half-decent QPR team, surely defeating a side battling relegation would be an easier task? In another piece of incredible luxury, the first leg was played away from home, on a Saturday at 3pm, and Leeds were given ten thousand tickets and an outstanding degree of trust considering recent events. This game was to be all ticket but the general public would have access to tickets too. The Oldham game had been the same but no trouble had been encountered, and so further trust was placed in us.

The only thing to dampen my enthusiasm and confidence was the venue: Selhurst Park. Leeds had had a worse record at other grounds but coming home empty-handed from Old Trafford or Anfield was understandable given the relative ability of their clubs. Selhurst Park, though, was the home of Crystal Palace: a relatively poor team who had spent most of their history bouncing between the top two divisions and never making a real impact on the top flight. At this stage, in their entire history Leeds had only won once at Selhurst Park: a narrow 1–0 victory in 1981 against a team already doomed to relegation. Even the great team of the 1970s had failed to win there. There was also the ground itself. I haven't been since 1998 and by then there had been improvements in the ten years since my previous visit, but at the time Selhurst Park was a desperate stadium: a huge open terrace usually given to away supporters, and two dark, dreary shed-like stands on either side of the pitch. The far side was little more than a non-league standing area backing onto a supermarket. Then there was the location. I have been to fifty of the league grounds in the country, including most in London, Portsmouth, and Bournemouth. None proved as difficult to get to as Selhurst Park. Either through London or around it on the M25, the ground is frustratingly elusive and takes an age to get home from. Charlton Athletic were at the time sharing Selhurst Park, and while our record at the Valley wasn't great either, this venue tapered my enthusiasm. This was my first visit to Selhurst Park and it's true that first impressions last. The only thing that made an impression on me was that Leeds fans outnumbered the home support by almost two to one; incredible given that Leeds were the club playing in the lower division. The ground was basically soulless, though: the open terrace lacked the acoustics for the Leeds fans to generate a decent atmosphere, and the Charlton fans, perhaps drained after a long, hard season of struggle against relegation, didn't appear to have the appetite or energy to cheer on their team to delay the relegation which looked to be beckoning.

The game seemed to encapsulate everything about the stadium. It was a dismal affair; in part, I have to say, due to Leeds refusing to take any active part in it. Billy Bremner, perhaps remembering his previous experiences there, decided to turn Leeds into Oldham Athletic. They barely crossed the halfway line. It was clear that Bremner was playing for a draw and backing his team in the home leg. This was not totally unjustified given Leeds' away record, and particularly at Selhurst Park. Also, nine successive home wins and no home defeats since November may have urged him to err on the side of caution. I feel that if they had gone for it, though, Charlton were there for the taking. They were adequate but rarely threatened and looked to be out of ideas until their striker Jim Melrose found space in the box four minutes from time and headed past Mervyn Day. There was no further action, never mind scoring, and we returned home hopeful but not entirely confident and with an aching sense of an opportunity missed.

We arrived back in Leeds at around 10.30, roughly one hour and thirty minutes later than a journey from North London would have taken. I read the match programme on the way back, and unusually Charlton manager Lennie Lawrence had some complimentary things to say about us, stating that if Leeds could overcome the qualities his side would show then they would go to the First Division with his best wishes; further evidence that opinions were changing. I had travelled to the game with a vanload of local lads whom I'd got to know through the lads I'd gone to Oldham with. They were borderline hooligans and very raucous on the way down, the van bouncing down the M1 as twelve adolescents whiled away the hours singing and shouting about the prospects of promotion, and taking the piss out of each other as only young British men can. The ride home was spent in relative silence; Selhurst Park does that to you.

I spent the journey home reflecting. A chance missed, but still in the tie and actually favourites to win. We were a totally different team at Elland Road and it was expected that Charlton would capitulate under the weight of Leeds' attack and ferocious support. As a general pessimist I wouldn't be drawn on that, but I felt we had a chance and it would be very close in the end. I was looking forward to the home leg with a degree of excitement I'd not felt in some years. We were only one game away from a return to the top flight, an end to the fractious and usually unproductive Yorkshire derbies, and a welcome return to Anfield, Old Trafford and Highbury. Not that these grounds were any more productive; in fact they were much less so. But there is much more glamour in visiting these places, and much less embarrassment at taking a hiding there. Also, for the first time in three years I would be going to work on the Monday after a game. Everything was working out nicely.

LEEDS UNITED V CHARLTON ATHLETIC, PLAY-OFF FINAL SECOND LEG, MONDAY 25TH MAY 1987

FINE MARGINS AND WORK POLITICS

The one thing I'd forgotten about working and supporting a football team is how you and your team come as a package as far as your colleagues are concerned. At home with friends and family it's a little different; they have a more detailed understanding of your life and therefore other subjects and problems with which to trouble you. (To be fair, as I talked about little else, my family were often anxious to steer clear of the subject of football and Leeds United.) At work, though, there is little time or need to discuss your personal life, and there is a huge distinction between friends and colleagues, even though in many cases the boundaries become somewhat blurred. Throughout my working life I found that colleagues were rarely troubled by what was going on in my personal life, but had a huge interest in my football team, whether they were interested in the game itself or not. Maybe it was because there was someone in the workplace whose weekends involved something other than Saturday-night TV and visits to B&Q. With rare exceptions, in most of my workplaces I've usually found myself to be the only legitimate football supporter. There were ones with a passing interest but who never actually went to a game, and others who had nothing but loathing for the game but still spent an unhealthy amount of time talking about it – usually in a derogatory fashion, of course.

I worked in electrical wholesaling for the majority of my working life, so there were also customers who were keen to discuss the previous weekend's game with me. This would save them the trouble of actually attending one themselves. Therefore, as the only attendee (and therefore internal expert), I usually had to give a minor press conference around twice a week. On Mondays especially, I was allowed to do very little before lunchtime. Being interrogated ruthlessly about the previous weekend's match was an exhausting experience; much more tiring than the actual work. Many fellow supporters will, I'm sure, concur, and will have walked into work on a Monday morning to face the immediate and inevitable question, "What happened on Saturday?"

What happened? How are we meant to answer that question? "Well, I went to watch a football match, and if you'd got off your lazy, parsimonious arses and forked out the three quid that I did, you would know what happened and would have no need to ask me such obviously fucking inane questions."

As I had been standing roughly one hundred metres from most of the action my involvement had been limited, and I therefore had little more to offer than what the scoreline told them. Yet the question was almost a demand and, having not been selected by the relevant manager, there wasn't much I could put forward as an excuse. Ask me why Leeds City Council's delivery was still sat in the warehouse and I could offer up a credible reason and take the responsibility and the resulting dressing-down that came with doing my job (or not, in this case). Ask me why Kenny Burns' defensive free kicks usually finished up in the top tier of the West Stand and I'd have little to tell you; basically, guys, because it was him kicking the ball and not me.

I was the first port of call for incoming transfers, even though I usually knew about as much as was printed in the local paper. When I divulged this, the looks of disappointment were obvious. How could I possibly not know about our recent signing of an unknown Dutch centre back from FC Volendam (Robert Molenaar, soon to be affectionately known as 'Terminator')? This was before the internet, but why didn't I pre-empt my colleagues' questions? Why didn't I leave my family behind, make a trip to the local library and find out about this new guy so the people at work didn't have to do anything themselves and would be suitably clued up on a player they had no intentions of watching in the flesh? Had I no sense of duty? Even better, maybe I could have taken a quick crash course in Dutch and rung Molenaar's former club to get all the relevant information so my colleagues wouldn't be left completely in the dark by my lack of application. Seriously, what sort of supporter was I?

I once went to our trade counter to serve a customer and found another customer there: a one-or-two-games-a-season man, who literally screamed at me that the previous weekend's game had been terrible. After a particularly embarrassing defeat I often wondered if I would get to work and be greeted by the entire workforce and customer base yelling, "*Copley out!*" at the top of their voices as I shuffled unenthusiastically and sheepishly down Shay Street in Little London to our premises.

In China, and especially Inner Mongolia, there are, unsurprisingly, no other Leeds supporters in the city that I'm aware of, and only one other football supporter (a Newcastle United fan) in my workplace. This is much better: there is banter, but we are careful not to take the piss too much as it could easily be us next week. I find this kind of stick much easier to take. At least they have no vested interest and are not supposed to be on your side. I have another friend out here who is a Stoke City fan, and as all three teams have their moments of astonishing failure, football is tactfully kept off the menu of conversation topics when one of them is going through a period of, let's say, transition. What used to really get to me were the people who would take the piss after an embarrassing defeat and then sidle up to me before an important cup tie and coyly ask about the availability of tickets. I would just gave them the number for the ticket office. These people, in the context of the lowest of the low, are only one step up from hooligans and racists, who are usually one and the same. Living abroad, I've seen two matches in the past seven years and I do miss it, even though I get to see every game live on an internet group due to my proxy server overriding Chinese paranoia about social media. But I don't miss that fearful walk into work on the Monday morning and the endless questions and piss-taking. I'm much happier with the slight ribbing from the Newcastle and Stoke fans. I've always considered Brexit supporters seeking independence from the EU to be akin to a metaphorical preference for a kicking from their father rather than the next-door neighbour. Maybe my case is the polar opposite.

This was my first day in my new job, however, so there would be no piss-taking from people who should know better. As an office worker, I was in a team otherwise composed of girls who had zero interest in football. This came as a relief as well as an unexpected aesthetic pleasure. After a few weeks I was transferred to become stock controller for a building site closer to home. Here there were a few other Leeds fans and yet again I was the only one who attended games, so the grilling started all over again, but by then the season had finished and I had three months' grace before I had to resume my Monday press conferences. I only worked mornings to start with, so I had plenty of time to prepare for the big game on Monday night. I attended with two old schoolmates, one of whom had taken the piss relentlessly after Bremner's first game eighteen months previously: a 3–0 defeat at Barnsley. We'd listened to the game on the radio and I'd had to witness his delight every time Barnsley scored and try to disguise my desolation with a petulant shrug and insist that our day would come. I made no effort to help him get a ticket and I took his presence with a smug, told-you-so satisfaction that made his staggering hypocrisy bearable.

The city itself was like cup final day. I had a very vague memory of the 1973 final and the mass of white everywhere, but I'd witnessed nothing like it since. Everyone seemed to be going to the game. People in shops passed on good-luck messages; others tooted their horns at passing supporters. The whole city, even the neutrals, appeared to be in great spirits and most were expecting victory. At twenty years old, as a seasoned veteran of a hundred games, I'd been trained to think nothing of the sort: football has a way of giving you nasty surprises, however stacked the odds are in your favour. I was excited, hopeful, and terribly nervous. In the stadium the atmosphere was incredible, with noise pulsating constantly around the ground. There had been almost double the number of people at Hillsborough, but nonetheless, here the noise level was comparatively off the scale. If the team were to go down they would go down with the entire stadium and, for once, the city behind them.

The game was just as tense and violent as the Oldham games, and tackles went in that these days would be punished with eight-match bans. Baird flung an elbow into a Charlton defender's face and received merely a talking-to. There was precious little football played, and when there was, Sheridan had a shot deflected onto the bar for Leeds; Charlton defender Peter Shirtliff a header onto the top of the bar for Charlton. That was it for first-half action. There seemed little chance of a goal, and Leeds needed one. Optimism was replaced by worry, but in the second half Leeds would be attacking the Kop End and everyone mustered themselves for one last scream. Nine minutes into the second half and young Leeds striker Bob Taylor found some rare space in the box and scuffed a shot past Charlton keeper Bob Bolder. Bolder's desperate dive towards the ball fell just short and in slow motion it trundled towards the net. The Kop End almost sucked it in, and captain Brendon Ormsby got a touch on the line to make sure. There was no real need for him to follow it in but after the semi-final heartbreak who could deny him his moment? Whether the ball was over the line is, anyway, a moot point. Leeds were level on aggregate and the stadium exploded. Looking back at the replays, I felt Ormsby was offside, but at the time I cared little and just joined in the pandemonium. This time there would be no extra time if the scores were level, but there would be a replay at Birmingham ten days later. With all keen to avoid that, the tie opened up as both sides searched for a winner. Buoyed by the equaliser and the home crowd, Leeds looked the most likely. They were starting to stretch Charlton, and they looked like the side who would most cherish a replay.

With only a couple of minutes remaining, Leeds came within a whisker of snatching it. Sheridan played one of his trademark through balls and Edwards was clean through, but the ball bounced and held up, with Edwards' momentum taking him in front of it. In one movement he turned and, in the style of Ibrahimović for Sweden against England, produced a stunning overhead kick. He connected perfectly and the ball sailed over the advancing but helpless Bolder. Everyone held their breath as the ball dropped towards the goal but cleared the bar by a couple of inches. Howls of anguish echoed around the stadium, and it was the last chance of the game. It was ironic that it fell to Edwards again. As I stated earlier, total delirium in which you have no idea what you are doing and hug complete strangers is a one-in-a-hundred occurrence. For it to happen twice in five weeks – and at the hands of the same player; one who at the start of the season had struggled to find the net – stretched the bounds of credibility to the limit. For it to happen a third time, just ten days later, would be *Twilight Zone* stuff. We almost got there, but not quite, so instead of a glorious winner it was on to Birmingham for Friday night's all-or-nothing game.

As we made our way home, a man at the bus stop asked us the score. When we told him he was unaware of what happened in the event of a draw, when we explained he said, "So why the long faces?" Why indeed? He was right, of course – it was still all to play for, but it was hard to know how to feel at that stage. Pleased or disappointed; relieved or frustrated? I think the Edwards chance made us edge towards the latter. If the game had petered out into a tepid draw on aggregate, everyone would have been happy to get to St Andrew's the following Friday. But having got so close, I could still see Edwards swivel and volley; I could see Bolder stranded, the ball sail over his head; and thirty thousand people willing it to dip in time and groaning in despair when it didn't. Edwards' attempt had been a breathtaking piece of footballing impudence; good enough to grace any venue for any team. But a part of me wishes it hadn't happened, so that, decades later, I wouldn't have to dwell on what might have been. People who call for more entertainment in football would do well to remember that for most of us it's the result that matters. I loved watching that Edwards effort and still do, but I'd rather he'd either scored or never tried it.

After talking to the man it occurred to me that I had a huge headache; something that had never happened to me before at football. The atmosphere, the noise, the tension, the occasion had got to me and the headache stayed with me until the weekend. At work I managed to hide it, but this was one of the occasions when I was glad not to be amongst fellow (I use the term guardedly) supporters.

CHARLTON ATHLETIC V LEEDS UNITED, PLAY-OFF FINAL REPLAY, FRIDAY 29TH MAY 1987

HOPE, EXPECTATION AND HEARTBREAK

The play-off final on the Friday night threw up another work-related problem. In previous years, getting a ticket for a big game was easy if you were unemployed: just turn up early enough and you were bound to get one. I'd sold my ticket obtained via my season ticket for four times the cover price, in the expectation that getting another on general sale wouldn't be a problem. But now I was working mornings, and although Leeds were given thirteen thousand tickets for the tie, they were long gone when I turned up at the ground just after lunch. There were touts outside the ground offering tickets for five times the cover price but I was reluctant. Firstly, the possibility of paying a hugely inflated price for a forged ticket and still not gaining admittance was not attractive. There will be those who will say that I deserved to miss out because of my perceived greed, and on face value it's a reasonable argument. However, I'd put the work in over the previous few seasons when no one else had wanted to know, including the treacherous but perceptive new owner of my ticket. I'd seen around forty games that season and felt I had more right to be there than most, and was suitably dismayed that I would miss out.

There is also something unseemly about those who seek to prosper on the back of someone else's loyalty. This has been a particular problem with cup final tickets and nothing is ever done about it. On the subject of loyalty, I had actually gone to purchase three tickets (the two others for the friends who'd been with me to the home game). I had enough money to purchase a ticket for myself at the tout prices but not enough to buy one for each of us, and felt I would be letting my friends down if I just got one for myself. Yes, in my shoes they would have looked after themselves, but it didn't sit right with me, so I refrained and went home. This has long been a problem of mine: I have to be what I perceive to be fair. I struggle to remember a single time when this loyalty has been repaid, but even so, I can't help myself. It causes me great consternation but also great pride – misguided pride, but pride nevertheless. It may be poor consolation to stand on the moral high ground but it matters to me. In retrospect, I didn't even tell my friends about the touts, and I suspect they would have balked at paying that amount and I would have been forced into keeping the tickets or trying to sell them on at the game. I also have to reflect on the delicious irony of selling my ticket for an inflated price and then being outraged about the same being done to me. False loyalty indeed.

On the day of the game, we all gathered in my bedroom: me, the two other guys, about ten others, and a mountain of beer. We also tempted fate buying a bottle of champagne. My house was open season and a sort of youth club until they all found a pub that would serve them and therefore had no need of my admittedly poor hospitality. The absence of morals in callow youth should come as no surprise to anyone, but these guys really were the pits and I remain friends with none of them. Indeed, from a group of around a dozen most had departed from my life within twelve months, and I found myself attending the majority of matches alone until my children were old enough to go; a situation I found much to my liking. This eventually transferred to my personal life when I started to develop interests outside the norms of the working-class boy. Now I much prefer to travel alone too. It may seem like snobbery but I feel I've outgrown my old friends. From being a borderline alcoholic, I now rarely drink and can go months without touching the stuff, so trips abroad for me are about history, heritage and culture, and not just beer and sun. I can get those things at home – well, OK, not the sun, but you get my point.

The thing about the rigid class system in the UK is that we are too keen to pigeonhole ourselves and let class dictate our likes and dislikes. Others then follow suit and see your personality as an indicator of where you are from and not who you are. People remember the good old days when football was a working-class domain and yearn for those bygone times. Personally, I do not. I love how football has become accessible to all classes, and people who complain about the ticket prices miss the point. It's simply market forces, and if people are willing to pay those prices then the clubs will be all too willing to let them. Everyone complains that ticket prices are out of their budget, but they can find those sums when they want to, or when the game or occasion is big enough. At the start of the 1989–90 season, when a group of us decided to get a season ticket as usual, I was the only one to end up doing so. My so-called friends claimed that seventy pounds was beyond their resources. Fair point: in those days it was a lot to scrape together, and I did it through doing a mountain of overtime. Yet twelve months later, for the same people 110 pounds was not deemed inaccessible and they all found the cash with relative ease. Had everyone got a fifty per cent pay rise that year to cover the difference? No – Leeds had finally been promoted and the club, which in the previous season had raised the price of a season ticket by only five pounds, had a reason for a more dramatic hike. Did people complain? Of course they did – they are Yorkshire people; keeping money in their pockets and their mouths open in a constant, complaining drone is what they do. Did they pay it, though? Leeds United's standing accommodation was sold out to season ticket holders within a day. So opening up football to the masses, whatever their class, was inevitable and a good move. Football stadiums are not the sole enclave of the poor any more than art galleries and opera are the personal pursuits of the rich. We are free to pursue what we enjoy, but we usually bow to peer pressure. For me, as my peers were becoming less reliable and, I have to say, less interesting, I had little need to fit in with them. I had already incurred their ridicule thanks to my interest in tennis and, to a lesser extent, cricket. I was also the only regular reader amongst us. I do these things because I like them, not because anyone else thinks I should or shouldn't.

This also happens in relationships. When my wife and I first met I persuaded her to go to games with me by saying that we were going somewhere with bright lights, lots of people and a fantastic atmosphere. She thought she was going to Mr Craig's nightclub and not a night game against Peterborough, but she showed a real interest and good understanding and I loved her company at games. During the last two years of our marriage we shared a season ticket. We had one adult and two children's season tickets, and the available adult took the children. She worked weekends and couldn't attend Saturday or Sunday matches, but she used the ticket for midweek games. If I wanted to attend at the same time I either bought another ticket in the stands or stayed home if we couldn't afford it. Yet when we got divorced and she met someone else, within two weeks she showed absolutely zero interest in football and one day when I went to pick up the kids didn't even glance at the TV when the highlights were on. Feigning interest for the sake of a partner is admirable in its own way but there is a limit. Pretending you care when your partner drones on about the latest managerial appointment, or having the grace to watch the game on TV when it really matters to them is endearing. But taking someone's ticket from them when you have no real interest is unforgivable. It tells you something about my loyalty to my team and my state of mind that I was more pissed off about her use of my season ticket than I was about her leaving me and finding another man. Kicking me out and moving someone else in? I deserved it; the marriage was over, even though I couldn't see it at the time, and she had every right to chase happiness. But keeping me from my one true passion when she didn't give a fig and knew the marriage was on its last legs? That was pure treachery.

In my own defence, when I was in my forties I met a girl at college who got me into art and theatre. We only lasted a few months, but ten years on I still go to see both on my own and have started to go to opera too; something I find surprisingly enjoyable. It wasn't a great relationship and was very short-lived, but I'm grateful to her for opening up this world to me. Now I love all these things and feel I'm a better, more rounded person because of them. I can't imagine them not being a part of my life. However, wanting to keep your own interests whilst developing others outside those of your normal social circle can bring its own problems which can be mildly amusing. A former teaching colleague from Canada found it difficult to comprehend that I had been brought up in a lower-working-class neighbourhood and been on the edges of, if not actively involved in, the football hooligan scene, but also knew who founded the Pre-Raphaelite movement. (Millais, Hunt and Rossetti, in case you're interested. Of course you aren't, you fucking philistines. There I go again, class-labelling and pigeonholing.)

Anyway, back to my bedroom. As was usual for the time, despite the game's importance it was only broadcast on local radio with highlights to be shown on TV later, so we found various perches around the room, drank lots of beer and listened avidly. Radio commentary is awful and I try to avoid it whenever possible. In an attempt to create excitement in a potentially dreary medium, commentators try to add a gloss of paint that isn't needed. The result is that even a team going over the halfway line at half pace is given a sense of impending doom and the promise of a goal against the defending side. Even taking this into account, Charlton seemed to be controlling the game and we silently prepared ourselves for the inevitable winning goal that would seal our fate. It never came in normal time, but we weren't fooled; we were not really in this game and even if it went to penalties, there was only Sheridan who could take them. Before he'd become the regular taker, Baird, Ritchie and Edwards had all missed from the spot. Unless Sheridan was allowed to take all five, there wasn't much hope.

If Charlton had scored early in extra time and gone on to take the tie, it would have been OK. Disappointing, yes, but over the three games they had edged it and probably deserved to maintain their top-flight status. You shrugged your shoulders – great season, great memories, but it was never going to be, so roll on next season. At this point, enter John Sheridan. Over the season he had made long-range free kicks his trademark but since Christmas had only scored with one of them. In the first period Leeds got a free kick just outside the area right on half-time, and the commentators got suitably excited. As seasoned radio listeners, however, we were not to be fooled and were barely paying attention. Only when the commentator screamed, "Sheridan... *scores!*" did we start to pay heed, and an almighty yell of approval went up from twelve incredibly drunk teenagers. My father, however, was less than impressed: as a rugby-supporting Castleford fan, why would he be interested? He ordered us out of the house and we danced down to the local park in delirium, carrying what was left of the beer and the fate-tempting bottle of champagne. It was on, it was really on; we were so close, just fifteen minutes from promotion. The second half of extra time was torture; each minute seemed to last hours. Seven minutes left and Leeds were heading for promotion. The beers were flowing, the champagne waited to be uncorked, and the party was ready to begin and last all weekend.

If a week is a long time in politics, five minutes is an equinox in football. Just as we were all starting to believe, Peter Shirtliff showed up. Throughout his career the Charlton centre half had had a goalscoring record of one every thirty-five games. Who better, then, to score two in four minutes and turn the game upside down? The first – a long, hopeful ball – played into the box and knocked back to him to stroke past Mervyn Day. Two minutes later, a powerful header from a well-thought-out free kick. Ironically, the man who would have been most able to stop him – Leeds hero and FA Cup villain Brendon Ormsby – had been taken off injured and would rarely play for Leeds again. The whistle went and my despair was complete. I threw the bottle of champagne fifty yards up the field and dropped to my knees, sobbing. Not a stray solitary tear or even silent weeping – open sobbing. I didn't have the strength to exhibit the anger I'd felt after the late Oldham goal two weeks earlier. I just felt gut-wrenching, heart-stopping despair. The champagne was retrieved by one of the others but I refused to take even a sip; it just wasn't right. Again psychology played a part in the same way as it had at Oldham. If Charlton had scored an early goal and won then you'd accept it; disappointed but deserved and that was how it went. But to be given a sniff and come so close, only to have it ripped away, was soul-destroying. The fact that over the three games Charlton probably deserved it and could feel entitled to another season in the top flight, and justice had been done, meant nothing to me. I was all about the self-interest, and only in recent years have I been able to watch the highlights of the game. For a long time the pain was much too raw. So Leeds were beaten by a team who normally wouldn't have had to play in such a game anyway, after coming so close, with two goals scored in four minutes by a man who would score only another thirteen goals in over five hundred games spanning eighteen years. Remember when I said what a wonderful bitch karma is? In a moment of excitement I may have overestimated her value. Karma is just a bitch after all.

There was one positive aspect to take from the game. I heard from friends who attended that, at the final whistle, some of the younger element had decided to start wrecking the ground in their community-serving way. This outbreak of violence usually spread rapidly, e.g. Odsal and previously at Birmingham and Leeds would have been heading for the newspaper headlines for all the wrong reasons again. However, this time the older Leeds fans were having none of it: they attacked the rioters and apparently used their own brand of mindless violence to get them to refrain. The rest of the crowd took the side of the older supporters, chanting, "You're the scum of Elland Road." The violence petered out to nothing and was thankfully completely overlooked by the media. So, twenty-two minutes from Wembley, seven minutes from the First Division, and absolute heartbreak, but not all was negative: things were changing within the club and within the usually hostile media.

There is a theory that football fans go to games to be entertained but I've feel that is nonsense. Entertainment would be fantastic, but this season was memorable because of the drama, not the entertainment. I've always felt that what drives us is the uncertainty. When I go to the theatre to watch William Shakespeare's *Much Ado About Nothing* I'm not screaming for the final curtain just in case something comes along to fuck it all up for Benedick and Beatrice; I know the outcome so I don't fret about it. That, essentially, is entertainment. Football is not entertainment in that sense. The semi-final against Coventry was a wonderful exhibition of exciting, open, attractive football that will live long in my memory. How I wish, though, that Leeds had won a tepid, boring game with a deflected shot. Even though the game was fantastic to watch, at the time I missed a fair portion of it. I was too preoccupied with watching the clock tick down while Leeds were ahead. I've seen Leeds administer a few hammerings and found them hugely satisfying, but nowhere near as satisfying as a late, undeserved winner; exactly the type of winner to which I had been treated at Oldham. When Leeds beat Plymouth Argyle 4-0 at the tail end of the season it was an incredibly satisfying performance. We witnessed a torrent of exciting, flowing football, well-taken goals and a truly dominant display against one of the better teams in the division. Yet it was nowhere near as memorable as the late winner in the dreadful cup tie at Telford. Those who demand exciting, attractive football miss the point of what's at stake. The semi-final and all four play-off matches were absorbing and contained late drama that will never be forgotten, but for the most part (and specifically the most important point) the drama went against us. I'd much rather it had gone our way in boring games which were largely forgotten because of the absence of dumb luck. However, if it had, I wouldn't be recalling it now. The Telford game was wonderful at the time but doesn't send a shiver down my spine in the way that Edwards' ultimately meaningless goal at Hillsborough does.

THE AFTERMATH, AND MOVING ON

Working on that Monday morning with people who had only a cursory interest in my weekend was a huge blessing. It was a long time before I came to terms not just with that night, but with the season as a whole. In its way and for large parts it had been magnificent. Leeds had played what I believed to be superb football and created a whole load of late drama with both positive and negative outcomes, sometimes in the same game. Hostility and vilification from the press and even fellow supporters from other clubs had been replaced by a silent, begrudging respect, and in certain quarters a little sorrow. A Leeds demise would normally have prompted unadulterated glee, but this time it was largely absent. We were allowed our moment to grieve.

The club themselves brought out a video titled *A Season to Savour*. They were sensitive enough to leave it until the raw pain everyone was suffering had diminished, but the choice of title was interesting. Is it really possible to savour something that ends in failure and heartbreaking, soul-destroying pain? Obviously at the time I felt it was nonsense and the club was merely trying to cash in on the experience. Yet in later years I've come to believe that it *is* entirely possible, and that the season probably had to end that way for others' attitudes to change.

After the Odsal riot, there were many who believed that Leeds had used up all their chances and expulsion from the league was the only just punishment. Outside the club there were few dissenters to this view, and the even-minded Leeds fans knew that the hooligans were slowly killing the club. The club had done more than any other to try to vanquish this disease, and there were certainly other supporters with as much bad form as the Leeds fans but they seemed to get away with it. But the fact that these supporters were a cancer within our wonderful club was undeniable.

It's fair to say that a change of success brings a change of attitude, even amongst hardened hooligans. It's easy to say, "They don't go for the football, just for the trouble", but that is an untruth. There are exceptions to the rule, but the hooligans have a good understanding of the game and actually do care, despite their misguided actions. This is not to pay them lip service; it is simply fact. But while most of us wallow in self-pity after a terrible result, they feel they have to channel their frustration into violence. It's horrible, misguided and stupid, but there it is. The fans with a reputation for violence usually come from underachieving decent-sized clubs. It's almost as if they feel they have to regain some pride by winning on the terraces as their team is so bad. *We may be shit, but at least we beat the crap out of you afterwards.* They know of no other way to channel their disappointment; that is their way to show their emotions and deal with the heartbreak. It would be much better if they could just feel sorry for themselves like the rest of us do, but not everyone is made the same way. I'm just thankful that I'm not like them. As performances get better the need to commit mindless violence dissipates and, as I said earlier, in bigger crowds the hooligans are less recognisable. So when in the first home game Leeds played Stoke in front of twelve thousand supporters, there were just as many hooligans as there were for the play-off final which thirty-two thousand attended. In bigger crowds they become more diluted and less prominent. So this season, when disaster occurred for the first time, it was in a crowd of fifty-two thousand, and for most the occasion was too much and the will to fight left them. On the last occasion, in a crowd of seventeen thousand, the older, better-behaved supporters took a stand. If only this had happened more often. So it was fan behaviour in the latter part of the season that was the watershed for the turning of opinion; a reluctant and turning of opinion, but it was there nonetheless.

Then there was the club and the football itself. Billy Bremner had Leeds playing fast, direct, exciting football. It wasn't for the purists who can only see the beauty of the West Ham United academy but it was skilful and good to watch. Even the Leeds-hating southern media started to acknowledge its merits. Finally, and probably most importantly, the most obvious reason for the turn was, paradoxically, the failure itself. Leeds were definite underdogs in the FA Cup semi-final and most people rejoiced at their defeat, but it was tinged with sadness after they'd played so well and got so close. There was also a feeling that the club would go up through the play-offs anyway and so gain the more important (if less romantic) prize. Also – and rival smaller clubs will hate me for saying this – the top flight needs Leeds United. That is not to say that they deserve to be there; everyone has to earn their place through the quality of their football. But the rest of the nation wants Leeds in the top division. They hate us, but to do so they need us there to hate. What's the point of hating something that's worth nothing? Remember the saying: 'Keep your friends close and your enemies closer.'

I remember when I first moved to China having an argument with a fellow teacher who was a Hull City fan and proclaimed that he hated Leeds because they always portrayed themselves as something they were not. His views were not without foundation. I also find it frustrating when Leeds fans believe the team should be challenging for honours based on a ten-year spell between

1965 and 1975. It was great but get over it; let's try and have other times. The accusation of Leeds fans wallowing in their distant past is almost entirely true, so I kind of agree with his sentiment, to a point. However, one thing is inescapable. "I can't wait for the fixtures to come out, so I can see when we play Hull City," said nobody ever. In the lower division, there will be clubs who will look to see when the Leeds fixture is before those against their local rivals. If not the first fixture, then Leeds will be the next one they look for. In the top division this is less so (probably local rivals, then the big four), but even after that I suspect that supporters will take a sneaky look at the Leeds game. The big clubs all acknowledge that they would rather play Leeds than Bournemouth, Burnley or Watford. At this stage, sixteen years was too long for a team of this stature to be missing. Now the club is back, all those in the top flight are enjoying our return. The attack-and-be-damned attitude of the God that is Bielsa is hailed throughout the division and the acclaim is somewhat disconcerting for supporters brought up on malevolence, but it's intoxicating just the same. For once excitement and success go hand in hand; until we raise our expectations, anyway. For now, we are back, and a welcome addition rather than relegation fodder.

It's bred into me to hate Manchester United with every fibre of my being and for me the perfect season would be one in which Leeds win the Premier League and Manchester United get relegated. The experience would be humbling for them and laugh-out-loud hysterical for me. I don't want them down there for too long, though. This rivalry is important for both of us, and although it shouldn't get back to the previous toxic levels, both sides need it and miss it when it is not there for any length of time. The first game I look for in a fixture list is that against the best club in the division or (if it is a different club) Manchester United. I can't get excited about a club we are not destined to play. People point to local rivals and geography for intensity but there has to be some sort of equality about it. Why would Stoke fans hate Port Vale fans when they never play them and are often two or three divisions above them? They actually hate Arsenal. This is partly because they see Arsenal as elitist snobs, and partly because they are successful and the footballing anti-Stoke. Arsenal are deemed to be all beautiful, aesthetic football but without the end product. Stoke, particularly under Tony Pulis, were the perceived aggressive, long-ball specialists; dull but effective. Arsenal are also from London and so carry the bias of the aforementioned southern media. Stoke City don't hate Leicester City, the other Midlands club with no credible rival; they hate a team from North London almost 150 miles away. I remember a Bradford City fan asking me why we hate Manchester United when Bradford are, geographically, our closest rival. I pointed out that geographically Halifax Town are Bradford's nearest rivals, so why didn't he hate them like he hated Leeds? His answer was out before he even thought about it: "Because they are crap, nothing, insignificant – what would be the point?" I just nodded and walked away.

In their way, the Stoke supporters are right. There *is* a lot of elitism in football, but their total disregard of Port Vale amounts to the same thing and we as Leeds fans are prime movers in this department. You may ask, "Well, what about Manchester United fans' attitude towards Leeds supporters? Surely they have the same level of derision?" Not a chance, obviously they have a hatred for Manchester City and more obviously Liverpool, they have not directly traded a single player with Liverpool since 1964. But watch any Manchester United game – on TV or live, whatever is your choice – and before the first half has finished you will hear the chant "We all hate Leeds scum." Even in League One, they were thinking about us. Thank you so much for the backhanded compliment; we missed you too.

Anyway, back to 1987. I always thought a better title for Leeds United's video would have been *A Defining Season* – less melodramatic and not as much of a sales booster, but nearer the truth. Ultimately, to build empathy it was important that the season ended in failure. However volatile you may believe they are, football supporters do feel this. Leeds were seven minutes from the First Division and twenty-two minutes from the cup final, if you want to put Edwards' overhead kick and Ogrizovic's save into the equation, maybe four inches from the First Division and a fingertip from Wembley.

You may hate Leeds, and many at the time were delighted by their downfall. But even the staunchest of detractors knew how they would have felt in the same situation, as I had at Oldham, and thought, *I'm glad that wasn't me*. So the neutrals and minor haters had some sympathy, and especially where promotion is concerned, many would like Leeds back again. For a while the general hatred was diminished and replaced by an awkward pity. This would not have happened had Leeds won something; in the British mindset the club needed failure to allow some sort of empathy for them to manifest. It's how we work. We despise failure in ourselves but empathise with it in others. Equally, we resent others' success and become coy when talking about our own achievements. Brave failure is what makes the British great and what we relate to. In 1987 we hated Nick Faldo and Nigel Mansell, both supremely talented but lacking in warmth and personality; yet we loved Frank Bruno and 'Eddie the Eagle' Edwards, who had nowhere near the same level of talent but plenty of that good old British trait of humility.

For a while Leeds had a nice kudos about them but, being Leeds, it wouldn't last forever and there would be times when both fans and club would again test the patience and earn the revulsion of the entire country. Sometimes deservedly, others not, but that is the burden of following Leeds. It took me a long time to come to terms with our two defeats and coming so close, and even now in my daydreams I see Ormsby passing back to Mervyn Day at Hillsborough, Bennett stood helpless behind him. Then I'm on the terraces at Wembley, shedding a tear as the Leeds fans sing 'Abide with Me'. Then I see Edwards' overhead kick dip at the last second and nestle in the top corner of Bolder's goal; I hear the Kop End explode with a noise that can be heard all the way across the Pennines. I see the team taking a lap of honour, celebrating promotion, carrying the FA Cup as they go. Most of all I relive those two Edwards moments that ultimately proved to be worth nothing. These are more tangible because they are real and I can find them on the internet any time I choose. The semi-final one actually means more, simply because it was scored in front of the Leeds fans and I can witness the explosion of joy, time and time again; an incident I was part of. The Oldham goal was at the other end of the pitch and so from my perspective is a little diluted, but still a treasured memory.

It's telling that I reminisce more than fantasise. For a football fan a sense of reality is never far away, but why should I think about failure more than success? I think mainly it's because following Leeds United has been largely a matter of failure, and the failures are just as much a part of our history as the successes. One of my reasons for hating Manchester United is their supporters' attempts to banish poor players from their memories. I remember an older Man United fan who was a regular supporter in the late '70s refusing to confess to the existence of goalkeeping calamity Paddy Roche. Mention Peter Davenport and there is quick acknowledgement before they move on to talk at length about Norman Whiteside, Bryan Robson and Paul McGrath. Don't even think about panicking them by discussing the dearth of goals from expensive reject striker Garry Birtles. In many ways this is, of course, the sensible thing to do. Reminisce about success – why look at the negatives? Thinking about failure cannot be healthy for the mind. But for a Leeds fan failures form a major part of our consumption and the history of the club. In my early days I loved Tony Currie and the ageing Eddie Gray – who wouldn't?

They were exquisite, talented footballers who seemed to be on a different wavelength to everyone else on the pitch. But I had a soft spot for Kevin Hird, too: a Jasper Carrott doppelganger of whom it was impossible to decide whether he was a class player who messed up a little too often, or a complete liability with a touch of genius. He could in one minute look like he'd never seen a football before, and then in the next smash a twenty-five-yarder into the top corner. Despite their inadequacies, Hird and others became cult heroes. They tried, and in a team of limited ability that was important.

So yes, it was a season of failure and it hurt for months, but there is a large part of me that is glad it turned out that way. It turned opinion towards us rather than against us, and, as Martin Tyler said, it was memorable and wonderful. The ecstasy, the delirium, the anguish and the pain were all part of a sensational story that I'm so glad to be a part of. Sheridan's free kicks, Edwards' joy-inducing goals, Ormsby's header against QPR, Ogrizovic's stupendous save from Ormsby, Bennett's once-in-a-lifetime interception, Shirtliff's rarely repeated goals, seven hours queuing for a semi-final ticket, the *Yorkshire Evening Post* going turncoat, the hostile tabloid press, even Emlyn Hughes and the terrible riot at Odsal. Good, bad, exceptional, terrible, amazing and sickening – they are all etched in my memory. All of them (apart from Shirtliff's goals) I witnessed live; all very personal but part of a wider national experience. Ultimate failure and no prize at the end, but an unforgettable experience. Despite the anguish and searing pain, it was definitely a season to savour.

AT MY WORKPLACE, ANY GIVEN FRIDAY BETWEEN 2003 AND 2012

In the field of electrical wholesaling, Friday afternoon is dead time. There's a strong tradition of electricians and other skilled tradesmen finishing at lunchtime on Fridays but this never transferred to the service sector so there's very little to do. Why we remained open completely escapes me. No one came to the usually overrun trade counter, no one called for supplies, and in the offices of the bigger companies there was no one to chase for quotes.

It was idle time for the accounts managers and we made no attempts to downplay our time-wasting. At the desk opposite me, two of the girls were planning a night out in the city; another colleague was on the phone, discussing a weekend away with his wife. Others merely whiled away the hours by indulging in small talk with people with whom they had little in common outside the workplace. At a nearby desk two lads had been talking about the weekend's football for some time and had now moved on to a good-natured argument about the finer details of a long-forgotten Leeds game. I knew what was coming next. One of them asked me to settle the argument. I did this with the minimum of fuss, and one of our newer workmates raised his eyebrows in amusement at my ability to so effortlessly recall such a minor, meaningless detail. (Whether it was Steve Doyle or Andy Payton who scored two penalties for Hull City at Elland Road in 1990, in case you are interested. The answer is Payton; Doyle scored one – a thirty-yard piledriver – as Leeds won 4–3. Sorry; couldn't help myself.)

One of the guys who'd been having the conversation looked up and said to the newcomer, "You think that's impressive? Watch this!" As he spoke he was on the internet, pulling up the results for the 1986-7 season.

It was performing seal time – not that I was bothered; I was bored witless and enjoyed the incredulous faces of new colleagues when I did this. I sat back, arms behind my head, showing no hint of feigned concentration, and began. "OK, here goes. Blackburn away, 2–1 defeat, goalscorer Andy Ritchie. Stoke home, 2–1 win, scorers Sheridan and Baird. Sheffield United home, 1–0 defeat. Barnsley away, 1–0 win, scorer Baird…" On I went through the season, in order, without missing a beat. Occasionally I threw in the name of an opposition goalscorer; a piece of unnecessary showboating, but still hugely enjoyable.

Two or three of my co-workers moved to huddle around the questioner's screen; partly to obscure it and make sure I wasn't cheating, and partly to confirm that what they were witnessing was really happening. Another colleague, who was on a phone call and the only one working, started to pay attention and ended the call abruptly, joining the enthralled throng. I know I didn't make a mistake – I never did – and I'm sure that this act has since been hugely embellished by those who witnessed it and still work there; no doubt to the point of me being able to recite every result and goalscorer for the past thirty years. In truth, at the time, I could do it for two seasons: 1986-7 and 1987-8. Before and after that I struggle a little; I know all the results and most of the goalscorers, but not in order.

I understand that this leaves a lot of questions. Firstly, how can someone who regularly loses the keys to his apartment and often forgets why he just walked into a room remember such minuscule and, it has to be said, pointless detail? Secondly, why can I recall in such detail seasons that ended in failure but not (at least with the same accuracy) the Second and First Division-winning matches? The first question can be answered by the fact that I care passionately. I believe there is no such thing as a good or a bad memory; just things one is interested in or not. Ask any person with a legendarily poor memory to recall the words to their favourite song and they will do it effortlessly. I have no interest in where my keys are and often lose them within my apartment, leading to a desperate last-minute search to enable me to get to my classes on time. Yet I can instantly recognise all 140 of my Chinese students and remember their names even out of the classroom. (They are all given English names, by the way; I'm not *that* good.) Secondly, in those two seasons, Leeds United were the entire fabric of my existence. Although I found a job towards the end of the 1986-7 season, I did little else. I got a girlfriend towards the end of the 1987–8 season but the relationship lasted only a few weeks; she was no doubt embittered by my distraction at the possibility of a late surge for a play-off place (it didn't happen). In those two seasons I saw every home game (league, cup and play-offs), and around thirty-five away games. There will of course be many supporters who have seen every game from those two seasons, but for me it was the most football I'd ever seen live and for the 1986-7 season, the most compelling; no wonder I can remember them so easily even now.

The two seasons of success matter hugely to me but I was less involved in them. I saw all the home games during the promotion season, but by then I'd settled down and my older son was born during that season. My younger son was born during the championship-winning season of 1991–2 and I only saw three games. So while I obviously remember those seasons fondly, they aren't as prominent in my memory because I had a life away from football and didn't need it to fill the vacuum of a vapid existence. I cared greatly still – in 1990 I scared my baby son shitless when Lee Chapman scored the winner at Bournemouth to secure promotion, and missed the rest of the second half trying to calm him down; his wails drowning out the radio commentary. In 1992 I danced around the living room in uncontrolled ecstasy when Mark Walters scored against Manchester United at Anfield and gave the title to Leeds; a song I smugly remember Liverpool fans singing for the rest of the game. On this occasion my girlfriend, having the perspicacity to realise what was coming, had taken the children to visit her mother for the afternoon, leaving me alone. This suited me: from the late '80s until my children were old enough to attend matches, I would say I went to about eighty per cent of games alone. Anyway, it was my day and I wanted to spend it with the one member of my family who really cared, so being alone for the day suited me.

Since then my level of support has gone up and down. I had a big resurgence in the mid '90s, then tailed off again in the early part of the new millennium. My appetite was whetted anew in the first season in the old Division Three (now League One), which almost bankrupted me and I had to stop. That actually started with a preseason away game at Burnley when Leeds were battling to stay in existence and I went to the game to say goodbye as I thought I wouldn't get another chance.

As I live abroad now, I've seen maybe six games since 2010. In the past ten years I've been to Tiananmen Square more times than I've been to Elland Road. Because of this, I have no recollection of certain Leeds players from the past fifteen years who are mentioned from time to time in the media or on social media. My obsession has decreased, though not become totally extinct, and I'm a better person because of it. I still watch every game live on Facebook – something I couldn't do in the 1980s – and obviously I still care passionately about my team. In moments of high tension,

I miss it greatly and have an aching wish to be at Elland Road. For me Friday-night games kick off at 3.45am on Saturday, and though I have class at nine I still stay up to watch them, then fight to remain awake through my twelve-hour working Saturday. The distance and the existence of an exterior life have allowed me to become a supporter rather than a raving, obsessive anorak, and the painful defeats don't hurt as much as they used to. I still celebrated promotion by keeping the neighbours awake for the entire night, but if it hadn't come off that would have been OK too.

There are moments, though, when I can't help but slip back and wallow in emblematic failure. I sometimes miss those players and their mixed attributes: John Sheridan's guile, vision, and fantastic free kicks; full back Neil Aspin's ungainly but effective charges down the right wing; John Stiles' endearing but ultimately unsuccessful attempts to step out of Sheridan's shadow; Ian Baird's flailing elbows, and his uncanny habit of arriving high at the back post for a header, looking like he'd just jumped off the top of the stand; Andy Ritchie's hard graft on the right wing to aid Pearson and Baird, and his failure to come to grips with the offside law. I miss the good, the bad, the beautiful, the ugly, the exquisite and the downright brutal. I watch the Oldham away play-off on the internet around once a week and Edwards' equaliser at Hillsborough even more often. Even now, over thirty years later, his perfectly placed header and the unadulterated glee of the Leeds supporters in the Leppings Lane End behind him send a shiver down my spine and make my hair stand on end. I play the last eight seconds of the clip over and over again, stopping just after Martin Tyler's famous quote. I never watch the games against Charlton, though; even now, that would be too painful. I vaguely reminisce about them sometimes, but only one moment. Every so often, as I did on the day at work when I was asked to recite the entire season, I close my eyes and see Sheridan's through ball hold up in front of Edwards. I see him twist and pirouette through the air; I see his spectacular overhead kick leave Bolder stranded. I feel him willing the ball to stay in the air as I'm willing it to drop. Then I screw my eyes tight shut as I remember that, yet again, Bolder got his way and I was left heartbroken. Then I realise that it was the ultimate defeat – that is why this season means so much to me, and why the national mood shifted to a reluctant acceptance of a team cursed by the footballing gods. Like it or not, history shows us that Leeds United have always been chokers; a team of nearly men who so many times have fallen at the final hurdle. It's become our default setting, and there were many more occasions when the same thing happened, although not in quite such dramatic circumstances.

I'm in a couple of online groups which normally focus on recent activity, but naturally history starts to enter the minds of the contributors. We football supporters can be a sentimental bunch, and amongst Leeds fans of a certain age this era prompts as much chatter as the glory days. Actually, it's what inspired me to write this book. Whether it's the football, the fashion, the times or a potent combination of all three, recalling that period allows fifty-something supporters who were teenagers then to wallow in memories of high drama and ultimate failure. Only sports fans would allow themselves to do this. But failure is a part of Leeds' make-up and is tempered by the possibility of later success. There's always next season.

LEEDS UNITED V YORK CITY, LEAGUE CUP SECOND ROUND FIRST LEG, WEDNESDAY 23RD SEPTEMBER 1987

THE NEXT SEASON

A horrible shambles of a game played against a poor team who were at the bottom of the Third Division. Leeds were mid-table in the Second Division and showing nothing of the flair, passion or drama they had delivered in the previous season. Baird had been sold to Portsmouth and Ritchie to Oldham and neither had been adequately replaced. Pearson and Edwards were nowhere near the first team and the striking roles were taken up by Bob Taylor and Peter Swan; both youngsters from the reserves, the latter a defender. Due to his injury sustained at the Charlton game Ormsby was out for the season, and Sheridan was trying manfully but unsuccessfully to carry the team on his own. In the second half York scored and an embarrassing defeat looked to be on the cards, until new signing Glynn Snodin, brother of the departed Ian, equalised for Leeds and restored some sanity but, to be honest, little hope. The goal was celebrated more fervently than most because it was the first Leeds had scored in five games and only their fourth all season. This was the tenth game of the season, and one of the other three goals had been a Sheridan penalty. Luckily, in that period only five goals had been conceded; otherwise we would have been in serious trouble. Still, this was not the high-octane football with which we had been spoiled during the previous season.

I'd started going to games with a group of local lads who drove to most of them; the same guys with whom I'd taken the coach to Chadderton for the Oldham game. This game petered out into a dull 1-1 draw (pretty standard fare for this season), and we trundled morosely back to the car. On the way home the others vented loud frustrations at the lack of a decent strike force and pined wistfully for the return of Baird and Ritchie. Sitting in the back of the car, I lamented about the romance of the previous season and contemplated the price of a season ticket wasted – another seven months of tepid, meaningless football played out by seemingly uninterested, passionless players to frustrated and distracted supporters in half-empty stadiums. The exoticism of the 'season to savour' was a distant memory and Leeds United had reverted to type: average at best, insipid at worst, and wallowing in self-pity. We could have been seven years from promotion, never mind seven minutes, and there appeared to be little to look forward to except another season of underachievement and abject misery.

Then the driver, Peter, distracted me from my daydream and asked me and the three others in the car if we wanted to go to the return leg of the League Cup tie at York the following Wednesday. The decision was immediate and unanimous. Of course we wanted to go – why wouldn't we?

ACKNOWLEDGEMENTS

Many people played a part in the writing of this book and it has been almost a decade since the idea first came to me. I would like to thank Andy for the initial suggestion that there was a book somewhere in my story, and the friends and colleagues who have had to listen to my constant droning about it since the first draft was completed two years ago. Heartfelt thanks, too, to the publishing team at Matador for their belief in my work, their professionalism in creating an excellent product, and their patience in dealing with my Luddite-like resistance to technology. My final thanks go to anyone who takes the time to read my story. I hope that if you are a similar age, it evokes many special memories.

This book is printed on paper from sustainable sources managed under the Forest Stewardship Council (FSC) scheme.

It has been printed in the UK to reduce transportation miles and their impact upon the environment.

For every new title that Matador publishes, we plant a tree to offset CO_2, partnering with the More Trees scheme.

MORE TREES
LET'S PLANT A BILLION TREES

For more about how Matador offsets its environmental impact, see www.troubador.co.uk/about/